the Beaded Edge 2

More Inspired Designs for Crocheted Edgings and Trims

Midori Nishida & CRK design

The Beaded Edge 2
More Inspired Designs for Crocheted Edgings and Trims
by Midori Nishida & CRK design

First designed and published in Japan in 2010
by Graphic-sha Publishing Co., Ltd.
1-14-17 Kudan-kita, Chiyoda-ku,
Tokyo 102-0073 Japan

English edition published in 2012
by Interweave Press LLC

First published in the United States of America by
Interweave Press LLC
201 East Fourth Street
Loveland, CO 80537-5655
The USA

ISBN-13: 978-1-59668-559-8

10 9 8 7 6 5 4 3 2 1

Library of Congress Cataloging-in-Publication Data
Nishida, Midori.
The beaded edge 2 : more inspired designs for crocheted edgings and trims / Midori Nishida & CRK Design.
pages cm
Summary: "Add the perfect bead-embellished touch to your designs with crocheted edges and trims"– Provided by publisher.
Includes bibliographical references and index.
ISBN 978-1-59668-559-8 (pbk.)
1. Crocheting–Patterns. 2. Beadwork–Patterns. I. CRK Design. II.
Title. III. Title: Beaded edge two.
TT825.N4953 2012
746.43'4–dc23
2012011503

Planning, production and editing:	Midori Nishida & CRK design
	(Chiaki Kitaya, Kaoru Emoto, Kuma Imamura, Kumiko Yajima, Noriko Yoshiue, Yasuko Endo)
Motif design:	Midori Nishida
Piece design and production:	Midori Nishida & CRK design
Collaborators:	Kanji Ishimoto, Chieko Ishimoto
Photography:	Yoshiharu Ohtaki (studio seek)
Procedure photography:	Nobuei Araki (studio seek)
Styling:	Tomomi Enai
Model:	Sylvia
Hair and makeup:	Yuka Murakami, Yumi Hareyama
Book design and Illustration:	CRK design
English edition layout:	Shinichi Ishioka
English translation:	Sean Gaston, Yuko Wada, Nozomi Wakui, Takako Otomo
Project management:	Kumiko Sakamoto (Graphic-sha Publishing Co., Ltd.)

Printed and bound in China

Contents

In the Islamic tradition, women cover their hair with a headscarf. Many of these headscarves are decorated with "oya," beautiful edgings made with a variety of techniques. This book introduces modern beaded edgings incorporating the beauty of this traditional art, with a focus on the Boncuk oya using Turkish beads.

Spring and Summer
The scent of spring and an early summer breeze

Traditional
Traditional Turkish patterns

Autumn and Winter
Autumn blessings and a preparation for winter

For Beginners
T-shirt collection

Story of oya
Enjoy some entertaining reading about oya.

Instructions
Let's crochet beaded edgings!

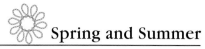
The scent of spring and
an early summer breeze

d e s i g n - 1
Gentle Cherry Blossoms

Instructions: see page 65

Designed and Created by Midori Nishida

Beaded edging for a cardigan

Select a fine thread to create the thin flower petals. Despite its delicate look, this flat pattern is a cinch to make. The tiny buds can be formed with only four beads fashioned together. Great pleasure can be found in the simple act of choosing beads. Let your creative spirit run wild and compose flowers with different hues of one color or explore a variety of different colors.

design-2
Tiny Little Cherries

Instructions: see page 66

Designed and Created by Midori Nishida
Created by Yasuko Endo/Kumiko Yajima

Fresh German Chamomile Flowers

Honeybees

Instructions: see page 67 and 68

Designed and Created by Midori Nishida

Beaded edging for a camisole

The German Chamomile flower is known as "papatya" in Turkey. This beaded papatya flower possessing a lovely three-dimensional pistil in the center appears charmingly life-like. A golden honeybee can also be fashioned using the same technique. Don't you find its striped bottom adorable?

Bashful Little Roses

Instructions: see page 69

Designed and Created by Midori Nishida

Beaded edging for a blouse

A tiny rose on the verge of blooming is suggestive of a little girl hiding a bashful smile. It's the outer petals that lend a darling rounded look to this piece. Simply space out the leaves and thorns to craft a chain to your desired length.

d e s i g n - 6
My Beloved Strawberries

Instructions: see page **58**

Designed and Created by Midori Nishida

Beaded edging for a mommy bag

Big enough to hold just about anything, this little girl loves nothing better than to carry mom's bag.

Why? Because it's covered in juicy strawberries, her favorite! Matching them is the tasty strawberry brooch pinned to her dress. Round beads of varying sizes were combined to produce this life-like berry with tiny seeds dotting the surface.

Sweet-Colored Sugar Candies

Instructions: see page 70

Designed and Created by Midori Nishida

Beaded edging for a camisole

Use a zigzag form to create the base braid. The braid in itself is quite versatile, and can be used as an accessory, such as an eyeglass chain or a strap, but here I attached little bonbons to the base braid using a technique called a knot stitch. This complex design is best suited for experienced crafters, but the feeling of accomplishment you will get when viewing the finished product can't be beat.

d e s i g n - 8

Summer-Colored Pincushion Flowers

Instructions: see page 73

Designed and Created by Kuma Imamura

Lariat

This pincushion flower motif is made by sewing double layers of blue and green-colored beaded petals onto a ready made ring base. These full and vibrant flowers are real eye-catchers. The Mediterranean turquoise blue imparts a refreshing coolness and will be the perfect complement to your summer wardrobe.

design-9
Fanciful Butterflies
Instructions: see page 74

Designed and Created by Midori Nishida

Beaded accessory

These expressive, flamboyantly-colored butterflies, much like you'd encounter on a getaway to a tropical resort, are made with vintage French jujube beads. You can also create chic black swallowtail butterflies by replacing the French beads with Japanese black jujube beads (see page 45).

*Vintage beads used for the piece shown on this page are available from the "idola" craft shop. See page 69 for contact information.

Popping Soap Bubbles

Instructions: see page 75

Designed and Created by Midori Nishida

Beaded edging for a tunic

This large motif, detachable like a removable collar, lends your tunic a versatile aspect. The front neckline is trimmed with a single layer of the base motif to achieve a simple look. This piece, which is a variation of the "Soap Bubble" featured in volume1 of *The Beaded Edge*, is known in Turkey as "manicured nail."

design-11
Spring Mimosa
Instructions: see page 86
Designed and Created by :Midori Nishida Created by Yasuko Endo

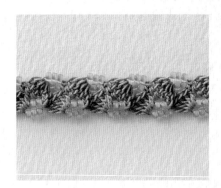

Beaded edging for a dress

The yellow beads represent mimosa flowers. If you are familiar with chain stitch and double crochet techniques, you simply need to twist the same motif over and over to create a braid. The edging gracing the neckline extends further to form shoulder straps. Why not experiment with different-colored threads or use various shades of beads to add an extra kick to the piece? Use your imagination to jazz up your summer wardrobe.

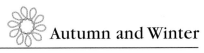

d e s i g n - 1 2
Arabesque

Instructions: see page 76

Designed and Created by Kuma Imamura

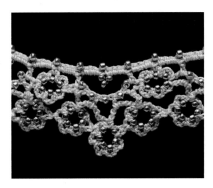

Beaded edging for a dress

This wide piece was inspired by Islamic arabesque patterns. The white thread lends it a pure and clean look while the burgundy adds just a touch of the exotic. This design can take on dramatically different looks, depending on the color of the thread and beads chosen, and complements the neckline of your dress just like a removable collar. Beaded picots of matching colors are also attached along the waist seam line.

design-13

Mandarin Oranges and Blossoms

Instructions: see page 77

Designed and Created by Kuma Imamura   Created by Yasuko Endo

Beaded edging for a crocheted vest

This is a fun design combining three-dimensional fruit and flowers adorned with little leaves. Slide on some small round beads to accentuate the natural texture of the thread, and weave them into shapes, allowing both ends of the finished strap to hang loose. Larger fruit such as orange and grapefruit can be fashioned by replacing the small round beads with larger round beads (see Espadrille on Page 37.)

Grapes

Instructions: see page 78

Designed and Created by Noriko Yoshiue   Created by Yasuko Endo

Beaded edging for a blanket

Piece together the grapes themselves first, then marry them together with leaves and vines to form a small vineyard. The sight of these dainty grapes swaying gently along the edges of the blanket is such a comfort. Why not pack it for an autumn picnic? Don't forget to take along your favorite wine.

design-15
Clover

Instructions: see page 79

Designed and Created by Noriko Yoshiue Created by Yasuko Endo

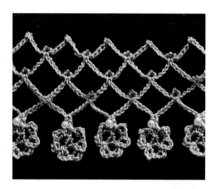

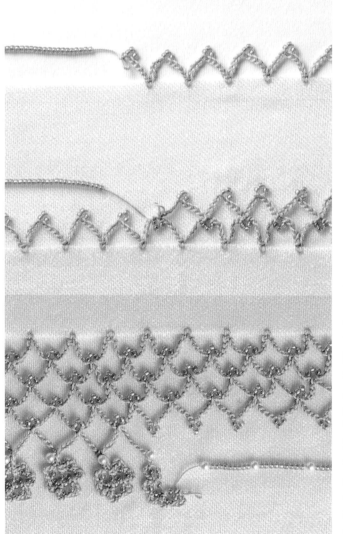

Beaded edging for a skirt

This net pattern woven with beads can be stitched directly onto the fabric of your skirt. Accentuate the edges of the net with beaded clover leaves. This lends your plain skirt a layered skirt look, and you will be tempted to do a little spin to admire the effect. This edging would also look great on the sleeves and hem of a cardigan.

Red Hot Peppers

Instructions: see page **80**

Designed and Created by Midori Nishida

Beaded edging for a tote bag

In the old days in Turkey, when a woman wore clothing adorned with red pepper oya, it was a sign that she was upset. Thus, the red pepper oya was a must in every girl's bridal trousseau, as a way of secretly showing her displeasure. Inspired by this story, I created these charming beaded red peppers.

d e s i g n - 1 7
Soothing Chamomile

Instructions: see page 62

Designed and Created by Midori Nishida

Beaded edging for an early summer stole

Chamomile tea is wellknown for its soothing effects, in the same way these lovely white chamomile flowers too have the power to gently soothe. Count each bead and slide them onto the lace yarn in order of white, yellow, and green to create evenly spaced dainty flowers.

design-18
Bright and Lively Scallops

Instructions: see page **84**

Designed and Created by Midori Nishida

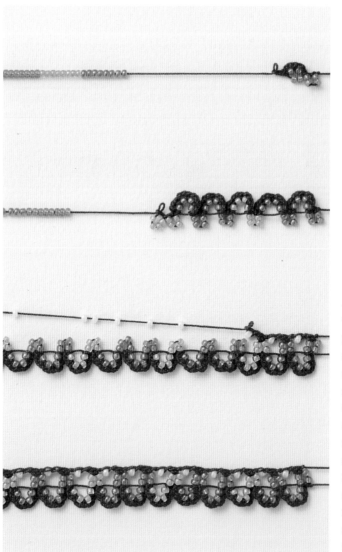

Beaded edging for shoes

This is a variation of the motif known as a "tooth cavity" in Turkey. The bright and colorful beads in four colors make a perfect complement to a Kalocsa-style embroidered skirt. Sew the scallops onto the shoes using a thick and sturdy needle, and you'll feel like a real cobbler. Scallops arranged into adorable flowery shapes are also attached to the straps to dress them up a bit.

design-19
Turkish Belly Dance

Instructions: see page **81**

Designed and Created by Midori Nishida Created by Yasuko Endo

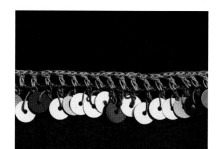

Beaded edging for a scarf

Belly dance is known for its fiery moves and the costumes the dancers wear are richly embellished with large spangles and coin-shaped light metal pieces that catch the light with every move. I created this double crochet piece featuring a dazzling array of spangles as a reminder of my treasured days in Turkey. Pulling out the guide thread feels like an act of magic.

Little Bird That Eats Red Fruit

Instructions: see page **82**

Designed and Created by Midori Nishida

Beaded edging for a scarf

If you have a soft scarf that your crochet hook can easily penetrate, it's a good idea to work directly on the fabric, wrong side up. That way, you don't need to go to the extra hassle of attaching the finished piece to the fabric. For a bluish scarf, how about creating little birds that eat blue fruit?

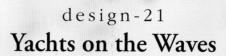

Instructions: see page **87**

Designed and Created by Kuma Imamura

Beaded edging for a cloth

The chain stitch represents the horizon, whereas the single crochet depicts the sails of the yachts gently floating on the waves. I came up with this motif while enjoying a peaceful summer day at the beach and gazing at the sea. The blue-colored sails represent the silhouettes against the setting sun.

design-22
Sun-Soaked Flower Garden

Instructions: see page **83**

Designed and Created by Kuma Imamura

Beaded edging for
an autumn-colored stole

This piece depicts a profusion of brilliant flowers on stout stems basking in the sunshine. Use fine, colorful threads to create delicate petals gently fluttering in the breeze. A perfect project for beginners, as you can work directly on the fabric and keep adding flowers at equal intervals by simply slipping beads into place as you crochet.

design-23
Dancing Fans

Instructions: see page 85

Designed and Created by Midori Nishida

Beaded edging for a change purse

Gazing at this delightful array of colorful fans, you feel like you've got a front row seat at a live revue. This motif is known in Turkey as "the pot handle." The samples shown on this page were created using fine threads designed specifically for oya. These little change purses are also convenient for storing keys and other items.

Beaded edging for T-shirts

The first lesson in remaking

Imagine how nice it will be to arrange your T-shirt in a beautiful yet simple style. Choose a favorite motif and decorate with the yarn and colored beads you prefer. You can enjoy re-styling your T-shirt as often as you like, simply by changing the edging. Here you will find how to handle beads, how to crochet and sew a beaded edging motif for beginners. Let's start!

design-24
Raspberries

design&make:Kuma Imamura

I got bored with this simple T-shirt.

Chart and symbols

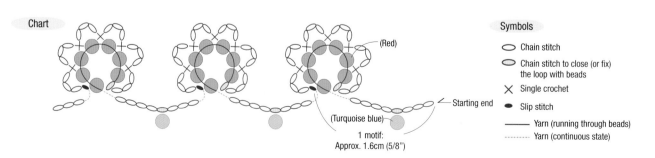

Chart

(Red)

Starting end

(Turquoise blue)

1 motif:
Approx. 1.6cm (5/8")

Symbols

◯ Chain stitch

◯ Chain stitch to close (or fix) the loop with beads

✕ Single crochet

● Slip stitch

—— Yarn (running through beads)

------ Yarn (continuous state)

44

1 Before starting, measure the size of the edging and calculate the quantity of beads and yarn required.

- 1 motif - Approx. 1.6cm (5/8") in length, 1.8cm (3/4") in width
- Length of beaded edging – Neckline: Approx. 57cm (22 1/2") (36 motifs), Sleeve edge: Approx. 19cm (7 1/2") (12 motifs) x 2

Material	Type/Product No. (color)	Amount used	
		1 motif	Total
Yarn	Olympus Emmy Grande <Herbs> No. 190 (red)	Approx. 40.5cm (16")	Approx. 19.5m (63' 11 3/4")
Beads	Round, No. 405 (red)	7	420
	Round, No. 264 (turquoise blue)	1	60
Needle	Crochet hook, No. 4 (1.25mm)	–	–

Once you've chosen your item, measure the length of the part to be edged with a tape measure. Arrange the tape measure so that the curved part can be measured accurately . The length of the neckline is 57cm (22 1/2") and that of the sleeve edge 19cm (7 1/2"). Based on the measured length, calculate the number of motifs and the necessary quantity of yarn and beads required.

Number of motifs

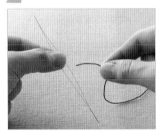

The length of the neckline is 57cm (22 1/2"). Divide it by the length of 1 motif (approx. 1.6cm (5/8")).
57cm ÷ 1.6cm = approx. 36 motifs
When the length is not easily divided, crochet extra motifs and adjust the length when you are sewing, or by increasing or decreasing the number of chain stitches or picots.

Length of yarn and number of beads

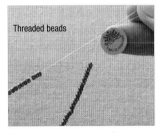

Multiply the number of motifs by "Amount used" for 1 motif in the table.
Yarn: 36 motifs x 40.5cm (16") = Approx. 14.58m (47' 10")
Beads: 36 motifs x (red) 7 = 252
36 motifs x (turquoise blue) 1 = 36
*The length of yarn and the size of motif in the table are for reference only. Allow 20 to 30cm (7 to 12") of yarn for finishing. In addition, since the length of a knitted fabric may be different depending on the individual, prepare enough extra yarn and beads for several motifs.

2 Thread the beads.

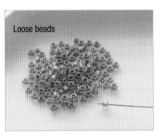

Loose beads

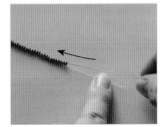

Threaded beads

① Open the center of a beading needle (see page 61), insert the yarn and pull it gently downward to fix in place.

② Since the beads are not yet threaded, keep them on a plate to avoid scattering and pick them up with the beading needle one by one.

③ Remove the sticker at the end of the thread carefully. Tape one end so that the beads do not drop off.

④ Hold the end of the beaded thread on a flat surface and pick it up. Insert the beading needle into the bead hole, pick up 7 beads and move them to the beading needle.

Threading the beads

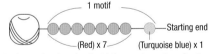

1 motif
(Red) x 7   (Turquoise blue) x 1   Starting end

Thread the beads from this for the finishing end so that the beads for the starting end come to the end of the yarn. Thread the required number of beads for the planned number of motifs, remembering that 1 motif consists of 7 red beads and 1 turquoise blue bead.
*Thread extra beads for a couple of motifs.

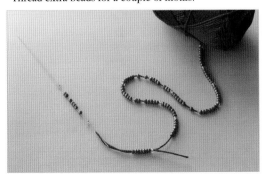

Which bead should I use?

3 Make a slip knot.

 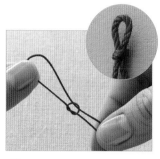 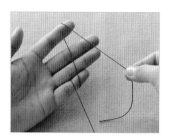 

1 Twist the yarn over the end of your finger and make a loop, then insert the yarn onto the end part. Be careful not to pull out the end of the yarn.

2 Pull the yarn in a loop to fasten. Allow 8 to 10cm (3 1/8" to 3 7/8") of yarn for finishing.

3 Holding the slip knot, twist the yarn once around the last finger on the left hand, then stretch it over the index finger.

4 Insert the crochet hook in the slip knot, and hold the end of the yarn with middle finger and thumb. Hold the yarn to stretch the part between the first finger and the slip knot.

4 Make 3 chain stitches and fix 1 bead.

 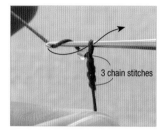

3 chain stitches

1 Taking the yarn, draw the hook backward to pull the yarn through the knot to make the 1st chain stitch.
*The slip knot is not counted as a chain stitch.

2 Make 3 chain stitches, take 1 bead and make 1 chain stitch (fix the bead with 1 chain stitch).

5 Make 4 chain stitches and close 7 beads.

7 beads

7th bead 1st bead

4 chain stitches

7th bead

1st bead

Make 4 chain stitches, take 7 beads and make 1 chain stitch (close the beads with 1 chain stitch). A loop of beads is made on the back of the chain stitches.

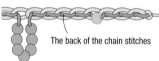

The back of the chain stitches

Take beads…

Tips

When taking a break or carrying the crochet, remove the crochet hook and safety-pin it. Use a safety pin also when you want to fix crooked crochet work.

Crocheting is a snap once you get the hang of it.

6 Make a loop of 3 chain stitches around a bead.

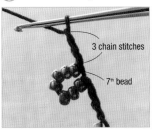

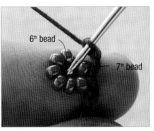

1 Make 3 chain stitches to form a loop.

2 Make a single crochet. First, put the crochet hook in between the 6th and the 7th beads.

3 Wrap the yarn that goes through the beads over the hook.

4 Wrap the yarn over the hook and draw the yarn from between the beads. Be careful to prevent the yarn on the yarn ball side from getting stuck to the beads.

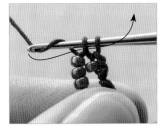

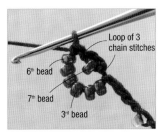

5 Wrap the yarn over the hook again and draw it through the two loops over the hook. One single crochet is completed.

6 A loop of 3 chain stitches is completed around the 7th bead.

7 As in steps 1 to 6, make a loop of three chain stitches around each of the 6th to 3rd beads.

Tips

Crochet a little tighter than when crocheting with wool yarn a choice piece. If your crocheting turns out on the loose side, try using a smaller hook. If too tight, try a larger one.

7 Make a slip stitch with the last loop for a motif.

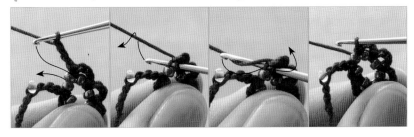

Make 3 chain stitches, wrap the yarn between the 1st and the 2nd beads over the hook, wrap the yarn over the hook again and draw it through all loops.

1 motif is completed!

8 Repeat steps 4 to 7 until the required length is reached.

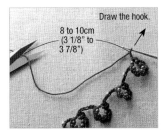

1 Repeat: make 3 chain stitches -> fix 1 bead -> make 4 chain stitches -> close the 7 beads and make loops.

2 When the required length is reached, make 3 chain stitches, cut the yarn and draw the hook to pull out the end of the yarn.

A raspberry motif is completed.

I'm not the best at sewing but I'll give it a try.

Tip Here you will learn how to sew beaded edging. When you sew the edging on a thick material such as denim, use a larger needle and fix the yarn tightly (for sewing instructions, please refer to p.85). Use a leather thimble to keep your fingertips safe.

9 Join the beaded edging using straight pins on a fabric.

Put the beaded edging on the edge of the neckline or the sleeve and fix it with straight pins. Adjust the shape so that the motifs look even.

Align the beaded edging with the hem of the neckline and join it using dress pins on the hem in the order of (1), (2) (shoulders) -> (3) (center of neckline). Join more parts on the hem using dress pins, adjusting the shape of the edging.

Place the beaded edging on the sleeve edge, allocating the red beads without loops on the edge. Link the starting edge and the finishing edge.

10 Sew the beaded edging onto the fabric.

Tip Choose a stretchy yarn of similar color as the fabric and a needle that can go through the bead hole.

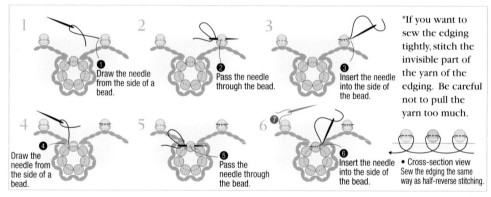

1

❶ Draw the needle from the side of a bead.

2

❷ Pass the needle through the bead.

3

❸ Insert the needle into the side of the bead.

4

❹ Draw the needle from the side of a bead.

5

❺ Pass the needle through the bead.

6

❼

❻ Insert the needle into the side of the bead.

*If you want to sew the edging tightly, stitch the invisible part of the yarn of the edging. Be careful not to pull the yarn too much.

• Cross-section view Sew the edging the same way as half-reverse stitching.

Make a knot on the reverse side , make a reverse stitch and move the needle to the upper side of the fabric. Insert the needle in the beads and sew the beaded edging the same way as half-reverse stitching (refer to the figure at right).

11 Deal with the yarn end.

Completed!

❶ When the edging is sewn onto the end, move the needle to the reverse side of the fabric and make a reverse stitch, then make a knot. Pass the needle through the seam allowance for a few inches and cut the thread, then hide the thread end.

❷ Thread the end of the yarn on the upper side and draw it to the reverse side. Make a knot and hide the end of the yarn in the seam allowance.

Color Variations

There are countless combinations of bead and yarn. Enjoy mixing and matching them with the color of a T-shirt, using the same colors or making an impact with contrasting colors, as if you were creating a mosaic.

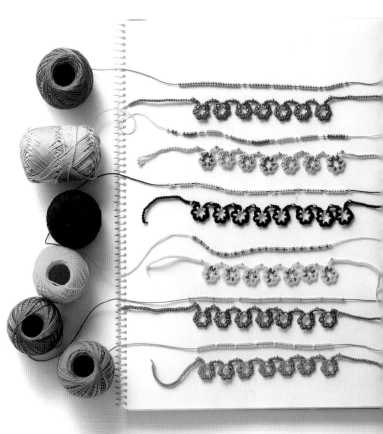

Pattern Variations

design-25
Lily of the Valley
Instructions: see page 86
Designed and Created by Midori Nishida

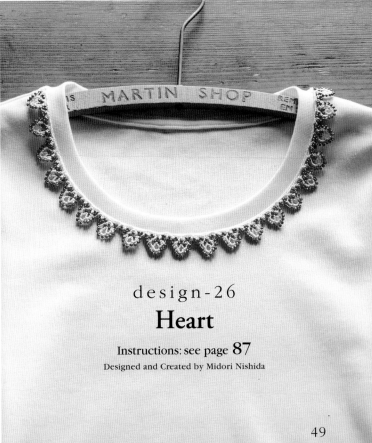

design-26
Heart
Instructions: see page 87
Designed and Created by Midori Nishida

Turkish Edgings (Oya)

Text & Collection:Kanji Ishimoto (Japan Turkey Culture Exchange Association)
Local photos contributed by Kanji Ishimoto /Photos of the collection:Yoshiharu Ohtaki

Decorative edgings are known as "oya" in Turkish. Traditionally, the women of Turkey covered their hair with a headscarf because in the Islamic world, it was long believed that a virtuous woman should not reveal herself in public. Even today Anatolian women still trim their scarves with oya, a form of traditional Turkish craft encompassing a myriad of techniques handed down from generation to generation. In November 2003, the Japan Turkey Culture Exchange Association and Bunka Women's University jointly held the Oya Exhibition, which was the first of its kind in Japan. This sparked an interest in oya among the country's craftspeople, who have begun to create their own oya and publish books on the subject.

Women making iğne oya in the city of Ödemiş

Sandık chest stored in the closet. A new bride filled her sandık with items she would need in her married life.

Types of oya

Turkish oya is made by combining floral motifs that blend into the scarf pattern as well as threads and beads that match the color of the fabric, and is renowned for its exquisite beauty. Oya techniques can be put into the following five categories:

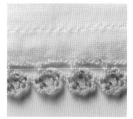
Boncuk oya
Made with beads using a variety of techniques. The one in the photo above is the "Bird's Eye" motif.

Tığ oya
Made with a crochet hook. Popular and easy to make, with a wide range of motifs available.

Iğne oya
Motifs are created by knotting threads with needles. The one in the photo is "Turkey."

Mekik oya
A form of tatting lace made with a shuttle.

Firkete oya
Hairpin lace. Originally created with a U-shaped hairpin.

Turkish oya and the bride

Oya is defined as "fine lace typically made with thick silk threads using needles, shuttles, crochet hooks, or hairpins" in the Turkish dictionary edited by the Turkish Language Association, one of the most influential organizations regarding language in Turkey. As stated in the definition, silk threads have long been used for making oya, but in recent years, due to declining domestic silk production and a rise in price of silk thread, the majority are now making oya using chemical and cotton thread, which are easier to handle. Also found in the dictionary is the phrase "oya gibi (like an oya)," an expression meaning "delicate, beautiful, and elegant." In the old days, girls accomplished in craft making were much sought after as brides. Girls therefore mastered craft making at a young age, and upon becoming engaged filled their "sandık" bridal chests with homemade oya. In some cases, a girl filled her bridal chest with oya crafted not only by herself, but also with pieces her mother or grandmother brought with them on their own wedding day. Oya was not only worn by the bride herself, but also given as gifts to her husband, his family, relatives, and neighbors. Turkish women today still maintain the centuries-old traditions of oya making, trimming their scarves with oya or sending oya to the market as a commercial product. A regrettable fact, however, is that in recent years the number of young females making oya has steadily declined, even in the rural villages. I sincerely wish the new generation of Turkey will embrace this artistic form of traditional culture, stimulating interest in Turkey among people of Japan through oya.

❁An introduction to oya motifs

Some oya motifs simply represent the physical shapes of common objects, while others may possess deeper symbolic meanings. People wore these motifs as a means of expression and communication. In other words, oya is filled with the thoughts and feelings of its creator.

Traditionally, plants, animals, insects, people, tools, and natural phenomena were used as oya motifs. A book on oya published in Turkey describes oya as "Anatolian women's language." Women brought up and married into large families wore oya to convey feelings of love, anger, hope, or joy when it was difficult for them to express such feelings verbally. The motifs made by young brides and brides-to-be in particular often carried with them a special message.

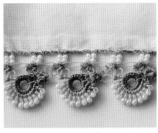

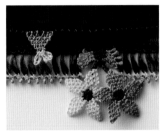

Hyacinth

A symbol of hope, love, and purity. A purple-colored hyacinth is worn during courtship and a pink one during engagement. The white hyacinth is worn by a single girl as a token of her purity and fidelity to the man she loves.

Rose

One of the most popular motifs among young girls, a rose oya is also used for decorating a bridal veil. The rose symbolizes infinite love and happiness.

Red pepper

This symbolizes pain and disgust. When a new bride wore a scarf trimmed with red peppers, it indicated her feelings towards her spouse were as irritating as a red pepper. Upon seeing this, her husband realized he has to work harder to patch up the relationship.

Apple blossom

Represents happiness and fulfillment. Being a symbol of the bride's joy, this motif is often given to those close to her heart, such as the mother-in-law and sisters-in-law. A new bride can also show off this motif to announce a child is on the way.

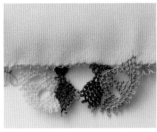

Almond

A girl wears a scarf trimmed with almond oya when she approaches the man who has stolen her heart to convey her true feelings.

Cimcime

This motif comes in two colors, one white and the other chosen from either red, pink, purple or orange. Cimcime, which means "tiny watermelon" in Turkish, is given to a petite girl who is as lovely as a watermelon flower.

Corn

This motif represents corn. It carries with it the wishes of the people for a bountiful harvest.

Carnation

The carnation is another favorite among young girls and brides-to-be, and is used to decorate the bridal wardrobe. The yellow carnation reveals their longing, affection, or even feelings of sadness.

Orange

This is one of the special oya motifs traditionally made with goat hair. Orange oya was specifically created to complement a young girl's bridal wardrobe, and is sewn onto silk scarves.

Casanova's mustache

Referring to the legendary womanizer, this oya is a form of social satire. Other similar motifs include "Turgut Özal's jaw," which is a caricature of the chubby former President of Turkey, as well as "Ecevit's nose" inspired by a former Turkish Prime Minister.

Soldier

This motif is worn by women whose husbands or sons are in the military. A young wife with a husband serving in the military is taken better care of by the people around her.

The origins of Turkish traditional craft lie in the embroidery created by nomadic Turks of the Mongolian plateau and Central Asia. It was in the Ottoman era that Anatolian women breathed new life into these ancient crafts and gave birth to oya. In this section, we will take a look at some samples of antique Turkish embroidery to trace the history of oya.

Beautiful-colored bath towel dyed with plant juices.

Both ends of the towel embroidered with the same design on both sides.

"Tree of life" motif

Prior to their migration to the Anatolian region of West Asia, the Turks followed a nomadic existence, roaming between the Mongolian Plateau and Central Asia. Embroidery fashioned by Turkish nomads in their tents has been discovered in the remains of ancient settlements. This early craft work was done on their tents and clothing as well as ornaments for their horses. Most commonly embroidered motifs were of animals and people, many of which were associated with their nomadic lifestyle.

In the eleventh to twelfth century, a group of Turks began migrating westward from Central Asia to settle in the region encompassing present-day Iran, Iraq and Turkey, founding the Islamic Seljuk Turk empire. Under the rule of the Seljuk Empire, the Turkish people continued to embroider animal and people motifs, but these motifs were eventually replaced by geometrical and plant patterns such as flowers and herbs. This gradual transition in motif design reflected the Turkish embrace of the religion of Islam, which forbids the worship of idols. The establishment of the Ottoman Empire in the Anatolian region at the end of the thirteenth century saw embroidery continue to flourish, as evidenced by the many Christian visitors from Europe who praised it highly.

Ottoman embroidery is said to have been devised by consorts of the court harem, who embroidered on silk fabrics woven in the court workshop with golden and silver threads, presenting them to the Sultan or treasuring them for themselves. These techniques were passed on to the artisans in the bazaars around the court, who began embroidering commercial products. Turkish embroidery thus spread across the entire empire, beyond the large cities to the women in farming villages who also began to create embroidery in their homes which they would then sell.

Products embroidered by artisans in the bazaars and village women were primarily everyday items such as napkins, handkerchiefs, scarves, sashes, towels, and other garments. Non-clothing items were embroidered with what was called "Cevre" (meaning 'peripheral' or 'edge' in Turkish), which was done on both ends or edges of the fabric with the same design. As Cevre embroidery gained popularity, women of the Anatolian region began making oya during the Ottoman era. It is not known exactly when Turkish oya came into being, but the earliest known reference to oya can be found in 1512, when oya was offered to Selim I, the Ottoman Sultan at the time, as part of his royal tribute. Oya eventually spread beyond Anatolia to the Balkan region, which includes present-day Greece and Bulgaria. Oya, called "bebilla" in the local language, is still made in some regions of Greece, though not quite as popular as in Turkey.

Pomegranate flower and fruit motif

A ship motif

A journey in search of oya

Text and report:Midori Nishida
Coverage cooperation:Kanji Ishimoto Local photos contributed by Midori Nishida / Kanji Ishimoto / Shizue Yatomi Illustration:Kumiko Yajima

The Turkish craft of oya (decorative edgings) had long been on my radar, but my first real encounter with it was at the Turkish Embroideries and Oya Exhibition held in 2003. Since then, my curiosity and thirst for oya has continued to escalate. Captivated by its beauty, I traveled across the entire span of Asia from east to west in search of oya. In all of the cities and towns of Turkey I visited, the people warmly welcomed me with, "Merhaba! Hoş geldiniz" (Hello, welcome!).

A ferry from Istanbul

The curator of the Ulumay Museum

Olive trees everywhere

Beautifully displayed iğne oya scarves in the market

September Ramadan (the Islamic month of fasting)

At 5 a.m., the sound of Athan (Islamic prayer) filled a city still shrouded in silence and darkness. This was in stark contrast to the night before, my first night in Turkey and first encounter with Ramadan, with people partying and playing music on the streets of Istanbul well into 2 a.m. The morning Athan marks the beginning of the fasting ritual. People fast daily until sunset in order to purify their mind and body and to be aware of people starving in poverty. Ironically however, one often hears that people actually gain weight during Ramadan because when the beating drum at sunset announces the end of a day's fast, friends and relatives gather to enjoy enormous meals together in preparation for the next day of fasting. It seemed to me that Turkey was not as strict when it came to observing Ramadan as other Islamic nations, and that people don't need to fast if they don't want to. Naturally, children, sick people and expecting mothers are excused from the ritual, and tourists like us were not affected in the slightest.

A wide variety of sweets similar to those in Japan

Stewed vegetables, potatoes, pilaf, salad, Ayran

Turkey is rich in great-tasting, inexpensive fruit

Sevgi Şenol, Yatomi and the author

Marching band members clad in traditional Efe costumes

Asuman wearing a bridal scarf trimmed with oya

Young people use oya parts as earrings

A tour of Bursa with Senol (Sevgi Şenol)

The city of Istanbul straddles the two continents of Asia and Europe, and thrived as the capital of three consecutive empires - Roman, Byzantine and Ottoman. It is a captivating city filled with a number of exciting attractions, such as the flamboyant Topcapi Palace, stately mosques and a bazaar crammed with stalls selling everything from gold, silver, and jewels to spices.

Rather than linger in this charming city, however, we decided to head south straight away due to a packed itinerary.

It was Ishimoto from the Japan Turkey Culture Exchange Association that put together the itinerary for this trip. Our willing travel companion was Y, with whom I learned the art of iğne oya in Beypazarı two years ago. She is an avid and experienced craftsperson, and her knowledge, experience and curiosity greatly eclipse my own. Y is so accomplished

Following local tradition, upon leaving the lokanta, the staff liberally sprayed out palms with kolonya, a volatile perfume with a refreshing fragrance.

Turkish fare is considered one of the three grand cuisines of the world. Everything I tried tasted great, but Simit (sesame bread) and Ayran (salted yogurt drink) were especially unforgettable. The word yogurt, by the way, comes from the Turkish term yoğurt.

As in many other countries, leaving uneaten food on one's plate in Turkey is not just wasteful but also disrespectful to the host, yet I found the meal simply too enormous to finish. Helping me out of a tight spot, Ishimoto advised me to place one hand under my neck, a Turkish gesture indicating that "I am full."

The trip to Ödemiş via Izmir

On the third day, we took a 5 ½ -hour trip to Izmir via long-distance coach. A crew member sprayed kolonya into

charms and to keep them safe. In wartime Japan as well, soldiers heading off to war carried with them "thousand stitch belts" embroidered by 1,000 women.

Women making oya

The next morning, we paid a visit to the Mayor of Ödemiş, who offered to give us a guided tour in a city-owned car. Apparently, the Mayor had asked the women in the neighborhood to gather at one section of the street for our arrival. A group of local women were already there sitting against the wall of a house. Spreading their collection of oya-trimmed scarves and iğne dantel all over the place, they gave us a live demonstration of oya-making. A bunch of cute, friendly kids also came up, peering curiously at the rare sight of a group of Japanese scrutinizing oya. We had often heard that people in Turkey are friendly towards Japanese, and those we met were no exception.

that she has even mastered the art of iğne dantel (needle lace works).

The three of us left Istanbul at 7:30 a.m., and arrived at Bursa around noon after a long journey by taxi, ferry, bus and metro. We were greeted with the friendly smile of Şenol, who was waiting for us in front of our hotel. Şenol was the lady who gave me a lesson on Boncuk oya 5 years ago in Japan. She has also published books on oya, which are of great value because books on oya are rare, even in Turkey. With Şenol as our guide, we made a tour of the city, stopping by the Bursa Folk Museum, the Ulumay Museum which has a considerable collection of Ottoman folk costumes from various parts of Turkey, and finally to the bazaar lined with antiques and oya shops. Everything I witnessed was new and astonishing. We then dined at a neighborhood lokanta (restaurant).

the aisle several times, and cool water and coffee were served. What caught our attention during the journey was the crocheted hat worn by a local man sitting in front of us. Y and I found ourselves deep in a conversation that would be unintelligible to non-enthusiasts. "Start crocheting from the center, divide it into eight sections and increase a stitch there, also making bobbles…" We then changed bus and had another 2 ½ hour drive. Sitting next to us was a lady from Ödemiş on her way home. When I managed to communicate to her in my awkward Turkish my love of oya, she took out her Tiğ oya scarf for us to admire.

At the Ödemiş bus terminal, we were fortunate enough to encounter members of a marching band clad in traditional Efe costume, and happily snapped some pictures. Their hats were trimmed with beautiful oya in a variety of colors. The Efe were local outlaws who protected the villagers. According to Ishimoto, the Efe men wore oya that their families and relatives had made as good luck

After perusing the stunning exhibition of antique embroidery and folk costumes at the Ödemiş Museum, we went back to City Hall, where two teachers from a women's vocational school kindly showed us their work. The "Belly Dance" motif featured in this book is a variation of the tiğ oya they taught us. I created this motif by weaving in spangles as a reminder of the cherished days of the Turkish journey. That night, Asuman, who served as our guide and took care of our needs during the day, showed us her vast collection of iğne oya, and taught us the names of various motifs.

Photo taken in Ödemiş, with Ishimoto in the center

A market stall selling scarves with oya

Saturday Vegetable Market. Vegetables in Turkey are all huge.

The view of the Ödemiş city from the hotel

A woman baking bread outdoors

Left: The oya-making lesson in the courtyard by Asuman and her neighbors was a delightful moment
Right: An iğne dantel veil. A pink carnation is worn by a girl engaged to be married.

The suburban town of Badem

The next day, we visited Badem, an Ottoman town about an hour's drive from Ödemiş with a population of 3,000. "Badem" means almond in Turkish. In spring, the entire town is covered with stunning white almond flowers.

A guest house remodeled from a 150 year old home was the only tourist accommodation in town. This historical house was adorned with embroidery, lace and felt craft, revealing the extent to which such traditional craft is an integral part of local life. In days gone by, women stayed indoors most of the time and sat by the "cumba" bay window, looking down on the street or knitting and sewing in the natural sunlight. My imagination ran wild, and I thought of how my life would have been different had I been born into this town in that time period. While home was a woman's universe, the domain of a man was the world outside the home. Even today, you can still see an exclusive group of men gathered around the table of a kahvehane (café), enjoying games like Okey, a Mahjong-like game, Dominoes, Backgammon and card games. Being an avid gamer myself, I was itching to join them, but couldn't because of time restrictions. Walking down the street, we noticed an old man heading towards us. Catching sight of him, the townspeople quickly set up some chairs and sat us down. Prompted by the people gathered about, the old soldier started regaling us with tales of love and war in a rich musical tone with a distinct intonation and rhyming. Perhaps he was one of the so-called "troubadours." The audience must have been quite familiar with his chronicling, but they seemed to enjoy his storytelling skills nonetheless, bursting into laughter, showing grief or letting out the occasional scream.

The day was packed with exciting activities, such as a gathering of village women making iğne dantel, visits to a felt mill, a Kilim studio and a lovely elderly woman who dyes fabric. It turned out that we were the first group of Japanese who had ever visited Badem.

The Saturday bazaar

There were approximately 30 oya shops in the bazaar, some in tents while others simply set up on a sheet laid on the ground. The most common types of oya found in Ödemiş were iğne oya and iğne dantel. Boncuk oya was quite rare, and the only piece I was able to find was a white gauze prayer scarf. Local shoppers are quite accustomed to haggling, but I struggled with this local practice because of the language barrier and a lack of experience. Perhaps feeling a bit sorry for me, one shopkeeper offered me an additional scarf for the price I offered.

A makeshift vegetable market was also arranged on the streets of the bazaar. Cabbage, eggplant, tomatoes, bell peppers, potatoes--all extremely large and beautifully shaped. People in Turkey buy inexpensive vegetables by the kilo in the market and cook them into preserves to prepare for the coming winter.

A Sunday lesson in the courtyard

Asuman kindly organized an impromptu workshop in the courtyard of a neighborhood house. Her neighbors gathered in the courtyard and answered our questions while weaving mekik oya and iğne oya at lightning speeds. Communication was by using hand gestures to conquer the language barrier. The open-air lunch of deep-fried potato and green pepper richly topped with garlic-flavored yogurt was so fabulous I had my plate refilled again and again. With much reluctance, we left the town and hopped on a flight from Izmir to Istanbul that evening.

Sevgi in the center

vegetables by the kilo in the market and cook them into preserves to prepare for the coming winter.

Our reunion with Sevgi (Türkan Sevgi)

On the final day of the journey, I took a stroll around the hotel with Y before noon. Truly two of a kind, Y and I found ourselves drawn into a craft shop, and shopped away for rare thread and needles. Waiting for us at the hotel lobby was Türkan Sevgi, our old friend who had travelled all the way from Ankara to meet us. Sevgi taught us the art of iğne oya-making 5 years ago in Shinjuku, Tokyo, and also joined us in Beypazarı 2 years ago, when we had dinner and danced together. There was still so much to learn from her, and upon parting, she promised to come to Japan next time to teach us even more.

A woman making mekik oya

Open-air lunch of potatoes with yogurt sauce in the courtyard

At a village café, an exclusive group of men are absorbed in games

Bay window of the Badem guest house

Yyarn, Beads, and Tools

Materials & Tools

The contact information for manufacturers is shown under the table of contents on page 3.

DMC
Cebelia #10-40 &
Special Dantelles #80

Both the Cebelia (#10-40), with its ability to harmonize among the family's beads, and the Dantelles (#80), attracting users with subtle beauty in a rich variety of colors, allows one to enjoy a multitude of color variations.
You'll feel dainty at the mere sight of the Dantelles' macaroon-shaped beads laid out in a line!

TOHO
Amiet

With this coated yarn, you can thread beads without using a hook. The Amiet has a rich variety of colors, from light to dark, and is recommended not only for accessories but also beaded edging of home decor and gifts.

Olympus
Emmy Grande & Crochet Cotton Gold Special #40

The Herbs' colors possess a gentle mood and the "Colors" offer a vivid flavor.
We recommend the Emmy Grande for beginners in beaded edging.
The Crochet Cotton Gold Special #40 allows for a shiny and beautiful finish.
Both parts allow you the joy of selecting colors!

Appleton
Crewel Wool

100% wool embroidery yarn with a fluffy and gentle touch. Its soft texture and subtle colors are very suitable for wood beads. One skein is approx. 20m (65' 7 3.8") long.

Kanagawa Oya Yarn (Tig)

From the special yarn in alluring Turkish colors and silk yarn with a lovely shine, to hemp yarn for leather goods and buttons, the wide variety of types adds to the enjoyment of beaded edging.

Kanagawa Orizuru Silk Yarn

Clover
Crochet Hooks "Pen-E"

A beginner-friendly crochet hook with a tip easy to thread and a handle fitting into anyone's hand. It is available in sizes No.0 to 14, to use with to various types of yarn.

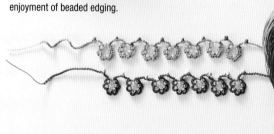

Kanagawa Leather Sewing Hemp Thread & Orizuru Tsurede

Tips

This is how to make a slip knot for crocheting. I recommend memorizing it for a quick start.

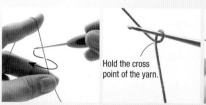

Hold the cross point of the yarn.

Wrap the yarn over the crochet and pull it out.

Close the loop.

A slip knot is completed.

Wood beads

You can choose the appropriate one from a variety of types, such as natural matte and washable beads.

Threaded beads

Useful for making beaded edging in one color, or using many beads in one color for a single motif. Make a loop at the end of the thread, join it with yarn, and the beads can be easily moved about without using a needle. (See instructions below left.)

Round beads (very small)

Round beads (small)

Round beads (large)

Pearl and Enamel gold

Loose beads

Useful when you would like to use a small amount of beads.

Magatama beads

idola vintage beads

The vintage beads of idola, a very popular shop in Kyoto, attracting customers with their beautiful colors in a French taste. (For contact information, see page 74.)

TOHO Beads

TOHO's beads are used in many examples in this book, as they are easily available. They feature slightly larger holes, allowing users to match beads with various types of yarn. Combined with your unique ideas, TOHO's expressive beads offer the excitement of making original beaded edging.

Kawaguchi Beading Needle

An extra fine type needle. You can thread very small beads with this.

TOHO Beading Needle

Responds to any thickness of yarn. A must-have item to thread beads.

Plastic rings for crochet and metallic rings

Use as a core for motifs. Concealable transparent types are also available. For a small motif, close the joint of a metallic ring firmly by using a nipper.

Safety pins

Useful when you want to give your eyes a break.

Tips

How to thread beads without using a beading needle. See the alternatives by using pre-threaded beads and an embroidery needle for beads.

Use the thread of the pre-threaded beads to fix the beads on the yarn.

Make a loop that can be undone at the thread end.

Pass the yarn through the loop.

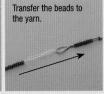

Transfer the beads to the yarn.

Use an embroidery needle for beads.

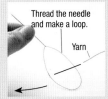

Thread the needle and make a loop.

Yarn

Thread beads and transfer them to the crocheting yarn.

All beads used for this book are the products of TOHO Co., Ltd.
E-mail: info@tohobeads.net
http://www.toho-beads.co.jp/

design-6
My Beloved Strawberries

p. 50

Beaded edging for a mommy bag

• 1 motif: Approx. 5.4cm (2 1/8") in length, 2cm (3/4") in width

• Length of beaded edging (6 motifs + 4 picots): Approx. 43cm (16 7/8")

Material	Type/Product No. (color)	Amount used	
		1 motif	Total
Yarn	DMC Cebelia #30/989 (green)	Approx. 80cm (31 1/2")	Approx. 5.1m (16' 8 3/4")
Beads	Round, No. 241 (red)	15	60
	Round, No.405 (red)	32	192
	Round, No. 164 (lime green)	8	48
	Round, No. 167 (green)	21	138
Needle	Crochet hook, No. 10 (0.75mm)	–	–

* The length of yarn and the size of motif in the table are for reference only. Allow 20 to 30cm (7 to 12") of yarn for finishing.

* Refer to page 87 to calculate the number of motifs required and thread the beads.

2 accent berries

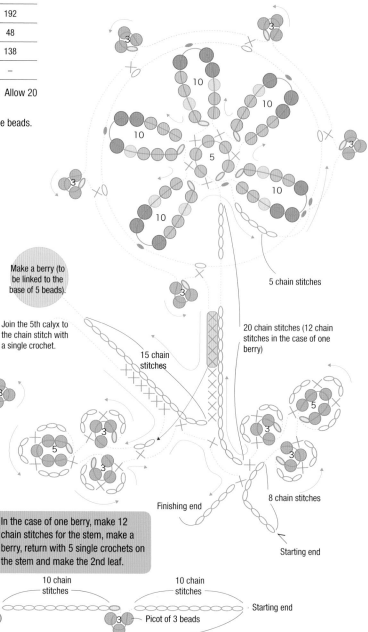

Sew 2 strawberries

2 picots

Ending picots

3 motifs   3 motifs

Make a berry (to be linked to the base of 5 beads).

Join the 5th calyx to the chain stitch with a single crochet.

5 chain stitches

20 chain stitches (12 chain stitches in the case of one berry)

15 chain stitches

10

10

10

10

5

5 chain stitches

3

Edging

18 chain stitches

5 chain stitches

* In the case of one berry, make 12 chain stitches for the stem, make a berry, return with 5 single crochets on the stem and make the 2nd leaf.

Finishing end

8 chain stitches

Starting end

10 chain stitches   10 chain stitches

Picot of 3 beads

Starting end

1 motif

Edging

Before you start…

Thread enough beads for the planned number of motifs, considering the number and the order. When threading the beads, a beading needle can be very useful. (Please refer to p.45.)

Threading the beads… Finishing picot (Green) x 6 → Repeat the following 3 times: [Calyx (Green) x 15 → Berry (A) → Berry (B) → Berry (A) → Berry (B) → Berry (A) → Base of berry (Red) x 5 → Picot (Green) x 6] x 3 times → Repeat the following 3 times: [Calyx (Green) x 15 → Berry (A) → Berry (B) → Berry (A) → Berry (B) → Berry (A) → Base of berry (Red) x 5 → Picot (Green) x 6]

1 motif

| Calyx (Green) x 15 | Berry (A) | Berry (B) | Berry (A) | Berry (B) | Berry (A) | Base of berry (Red) x 5 | Picot (Green) x 6 |

(A)

(B)

(Lime green) Round bead (red) (Red)

End of yarn at the starting end

◆ Starting … Make picots.

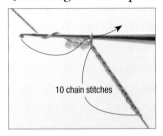

10 chain stitches

1 Make a slip knot and 10 chain stitches, then take 3 beads.

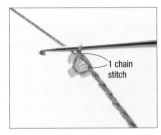

1 chain stitch

2 Close the 3 beads in step 1 with a chain stitch. 1 picot is completed.

◆ Make a base for a berry.

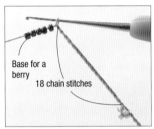

Base for a berry

18 chain stitches

3 Repeat steps 1 to 2 to make 2 picots. Then make 18 chain stitches and take 5 beads.

4 Close the 5 beads in step 3 with a chain stitch. This is the base for a berry.

◆ Make berries around the base.

5 Take 10 beads and close them with 1 chain stitch.

6 The photo shows the closed beads.

7 Turn around the berry to curve it to the right.

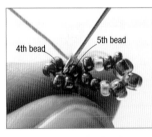

4th bead   5th bead

8 Put the crochet hook in between the 4th and 5th beads and wrap the yarn going through the beads over the hook.

9 Make a single crochet on the yarn wrapped in step 8.

10 A single crochet is made, and one berry is linked to the base. Repeat steps 5 to 9 four more times.

11 Five berries are linked to the base. Take down the starting chain stitches to the front.

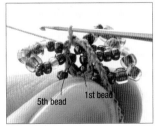

5th bead   1st bead

12 Wrap the yarn in between the 5th and 1st beads over the hook across the chain stitches in step 11 and make a slip stitch.

◆ Make a three-dimensional berry.

13 Make 5 chain stitches (these chain stitches will be hidden in the berry motif).

14 Make a slip stitch in between the 5th and 6th beads of the 1st berry.

15 Make 1 chain stitch, and wrap the yarn in between the 5th and 6th beads of the next berry over the hook.

16 Repeat steps 14 to 15 to join the berry parts.

◆ Make berries around the base.

17 Take 10 beads and close them with 1 chain stitch.

18 The photo shows the closed beads.

A three-dimensional berry is completed.

◆ Make calyxes.

19 Take 3 beads and close it with a chain stitch.

20 The 3 beads are closed. Then make a single crochet while wrapping around the chain stitch in step 15.

21 A single crochet is made. Then a calyx is completed. Repeat steps 19 to 20 to make 4 more calyxes.

22 Five calyxes are made and a berry is completed.

◆ Make the stem with single crochets.

23 Make single crochets while wrapping around the chain stitches sticking out from the center of the berry.

24 Make 3 single crochets in total.

1 motif is completed!

Repeat steps from 10 chain stitches in step 1 to the required length.

Two accent berries

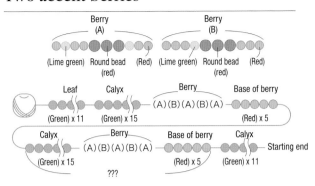

Berry (A) — (Lime green) Round bead (red) (Red)

Berry (B) — (Lime green) Round bead (red) (Red)

Leaf (Green) x 11 — Calyx (Green) x 15 — Berry (A)(B)(A)(B)(A) — Base of berry (Red) x 5

Calyx (Green) x 15 — Berry (A)(B)(A)(B)(A) — Base of berry (Red) x 5 — Calyx (Green) x 11 — Starting end

???

◆ Make the 1st leaf.

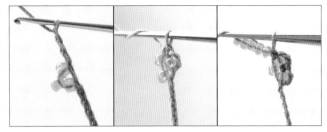

1 Make a slip knot. Make 8 chain stitches, close 3 beads with a chain stitch, make 3 chain stitches and make a single crochet at the yarn in between the 2nd and 3rd beads. Make 3 chain stitches, then make a loop around the 2nd bead.

2 Take 5 beads and close it with a chain stitch, and make the loops of 3 chain stitches around the 4th and 5th beads, then around the 3rd bead, and around the 1st and 2nd beads.

3 Take 3 beads and close it with a chain stitch, and make the loops of 3 chain stitches around the 3rd and 2nd beads.

4 Make a single crochet while wrapping around the 8 chain stitches of step 1 to assemble the leaf.

5 One leaf is completed.

◆ Make 2 berries.

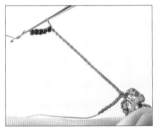

6 Make 20 chain stitches, and crochet 1 berry as shown on page 59 (step 3) to 60 (step 22).

7 Make 10 single crochets while wrapping around the 20 chain stitches in step 6 to make the stem.

8 Make 15 chain stitches, make a berry in the same way as step 6 and make 6 single crochets using the chain stitches.

◆ Make the 2nd leaf.

9 Five calyxes are made and a berry is completed.

◆ Assemble the berries and leaves.

Make a single crochet at ★.

Make a single crochet at ☆.

10 Make a single crochet while wrapping around the 2 chain stitches in step 9 to put the leaves together. Then make single crochets while wrapping around the chain stitch at ★ (in between the berries) and at ☆ (in between the berry and the 1st leaf).

11 Make a single crochet while wrapping around the first chain stitch in step 1 to put together the leaves and berries, and make 5 chain stitches.

Completed.

design-17
Soothing Chamomile

Early summer stole

- Size: 60cm (23 5/8") x 180cm (70 7/8") • 1 motif: Approx. 3cm (1 1/8")
- Length of beaded edging: Approx. 180cm (70 7/8") (60 motifs) x 2

Material	Type/Product No. (color)	Amount used		
		1 motif	10 motifs	Total (120 motifs)
Yarn	DMC Cebelia #40 BLANC (white)	Approx. 110.5cm (43 1/2")	Approx. 11.05m (36' 1 1/4")	Approx. 132m (433' 7/8")
Beads	Round, No. 947 (green)	28	280	3360
	Round, No. 102 (yellow)	6	60	720
	Round, No. 121 (white)	18	180	2160
Needle	Crochet hook, No. 10 (0.75mm)	–	–	–

* The length of yarn and the size of motif in the table are for reference only. Allow 20 to 30cm (7 to 12") of yarn for finishing.
* Refer to page 44 for symbols.

1st row

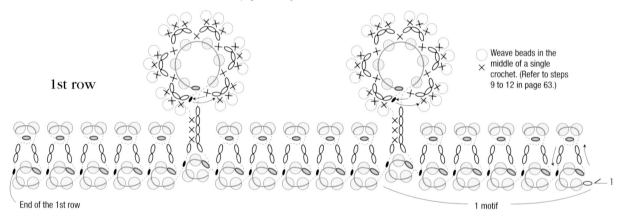

○ Weave beads in the middle of a single crochet. (Refer to steps 9 to 12 in page 63.)

End of the 1st row

1 motif

2nd row

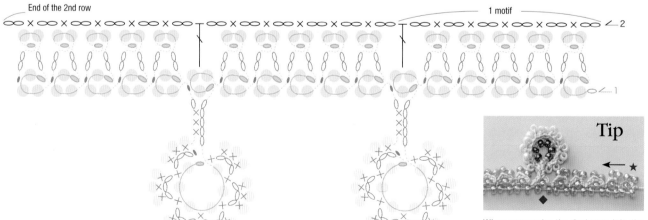

End of the 2nd row

1 motif

Tip

When you make the 2nd row, join the yarn at ★ and crochet in the direction of the arrow. Take down the flower motif from the other side as shown in the chart when you make a double crochet at ◆ (refer to step 21 on p.64).

Before you start…

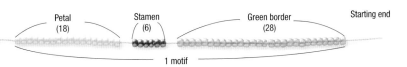

Petal
(18)

Stamen
(6)

Green border
(28)

Starting end

1 motif

* To clarify instructions, different colors are used for the beads and yarn.

Thread enough beads for the planned number of motifs, considering the number and the order.
When you use beads of multiple colors, use a beading needle.
(Please refer to p.45 for instructions.)
Threading order for 1 motif … 18 beads for petal → 6 beads for the stamen → 28 beads for green border (52 beads in total)

◆ Crochet a green border.

1 ake a slip knot and a chain stitch, then take 3 beads and close it with a chain stitch.

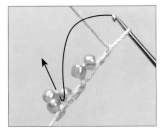

2 Make 2 chain stitches, take 2 beads and close it with a chain stitch, then make 2 chain stitches. Insert the hook between the 2nd and the 3rd beads of step 1.

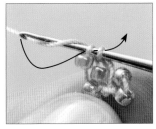

3 Wrap the yarn over the hook and make a slip stitch.

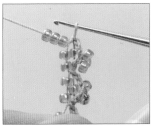

4 Repeat steps 1 to 3 (except the slip knot and a chain stitch), take 3 beads and close it with a chain stitch.

◆ Crochet the stamen.

5 Make 5 chain stitches for the stem, take 6 beads and close it with a chain stitch to make a loop.

6 Turn the flower around, make 3 chain stitches, make a single crochet in between the beads (crochet looking at the reverse side) to make a loop around a bead in the stamen part.

7 Loops are made around the 6 beads.

8 Make a slip stitch at the 1st loop and turn the flower around again.

◆ Make petals.

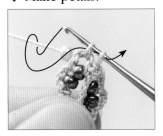

9 Wrap the yarn over the hook from the 6th loop, take 1 bead and wrap the yarn over the hook again, and draw the hook through all loops.

10 A bead is crocheted on the reverse side of the single crochet.

11 Repeat steps 9 to 10 to add 3 beads to 1 loop with single crochets.

12 Each loop has 3 beads.

◆ Make single crochets using the stem.

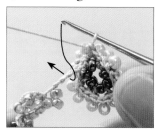

13 Make 3 single crochets while wrapping around the chain stitches of the stem.

14 Three single crochets are formed.

15 Make a chain stitch, then make a slip stitch in between the 2nd and 3rd beads closed in step 4.

1 motif of the 1st row is completed!

◆ Make the border of the 2nd motif.

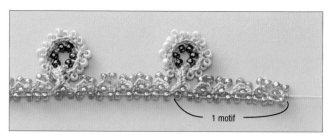

16 In the same way as the 1st motif, take 3 beads and close it with a chain stitch.

17 Make 2 chain stitches, take 2 beads and close it with a chain stitch, and make 2 chain stitches. Make a slip stitch in between the 2nd and the 3rd beads of the 3 beads.

18 Make the border with 28 beads, then make a flower motif. Repeat these steps until the required number of motifs is reached, crochet the border for 1 motif (the last 3 beads are not necessary), and cut the yarn.

1 motif

◆ Make the 2nd row.

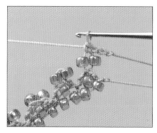

19 Make a slip knot and 2 chain stitches with another piece of yarn, and insert the hook in between the 2 beads of the 1st row.

20 Make a single crochet in between the 2 beads.

21 Repeat [2 chain stitches -> single crochet] up to the neck of the flower motif, and take down the flower motif to the other side.

22 Make 2 chain stitches, and make a double crochet in between the 3 beads.

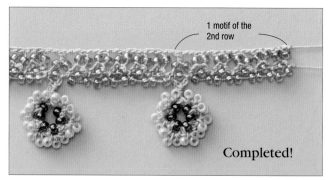

23 After the double crochet is made, raise the border from the other side.

24 Repeat [2 chain stitches -> single crochet] up to the end of the row, make 2 chain stitches and cut the yarn.

1 motif of the 2nd row

Completed!

Gentle Cherry Blossoms

Beaded edging for a cardigan

p. 4

- 1 motif: Approx. 5cm (2") in length, 1.7cm (5/8") in width
- Length of beaded edging (12 motifs + 2 buds): Approx. 62.5cm (24 5/8")

Material	Type/Product No. (color)	Amount used		
		1 motif	10 motifs	Total
Yarn	DMC Special Dentelles #80/818 (pink)	Approx. 1m (39 3/8")	Approx. 10m (32' 9 3/4")	Approx. 12.2m (40' 3/8")
Beads	Round, No.911 (pink)	24	240	292
	Round, No.246 (green)	4	40	52
	Round, No.121 (white)	5	50	60
Needle	Crochet hook, No. 10 (0.75mm)	–	–	–

* The length of yarn and the size of motif in the table are for reference only. Allow 20 to 30cm (7 to 12") of yarn for finishing.

Threading the beads

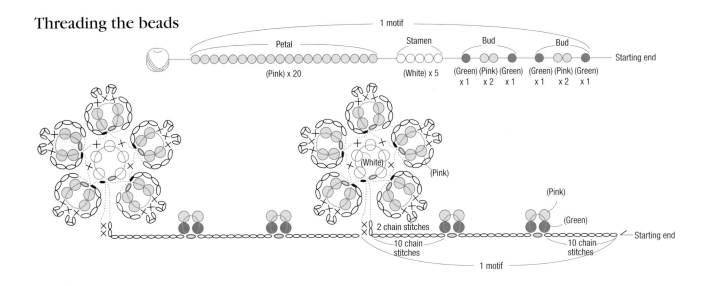

1   Refer to page 84 to calculate the number of motifs required. Since the crocheted work may be shorter than the size shown above, prepare extra beads for a couple of motifs.

2   Thread the beads onto the yarn as shown above and make a starting stitch for the 1st row.

3   Make 10 chain stitches, take 4 beads and close it with a chain stitch. Repeat these steps again to make 2 picots of buds.

4   Make 12 chain stitches, take 5 beads and close it with a chain stitch to make a stamen.

5   Take 4 beads and close it with a chain stitch, then make 4 chain stitches and make a single crochet at the yarn in between the beads to make a loop.

6   Make 3 chain stitches and make a single crochet at the same point. Repeat these steps again to make 2 small loops on the edge of the petal.

7   Make 4 chain stitches and draw it through the yarn at the base of the beads to fix the loop, and make a single crochet at the yarn in between the beads at the stamen.

8   Repeat steps 5 to 7 to make 5 petals in total. When you make the 5th petal, fix the loop to the yarn in between the beads with a slip stitch.

9   Make 2 single crochets while wrapping around the chain stitches (stem) in step 4. 1 motif is completed.

Tiny Little Cherries

Beaded edging for children's clothing, baby shoes and candle holders

- 1 cherry: Approx. 2cm (3/4") in length and width
- 1 picot: Approx. 2cm (3/4") in length

p.6

Material	Type/Product No. (color)	Amount used	
		1 cherry	1 picot
Yarn	DMC Special Dentelles #80 A/C: No.368 (light green) B: No.3052 (moss green)	Approx. 1m (39 3/8")	Approx. 8cm (3 1/8")
Beads	Round, A/B: No.332 (purple-red) C: No.165 (red)	70	3
	Round, A/B/C: No.167 (green)	18	-
Needle	Crochet hook, No. 10 (0.75mm)	–	–

* The length of yarn and the size of motif in the table are for reference only. Allow 20 to 30cm (7 to 12") of yarn for finishing.

Threading the beads

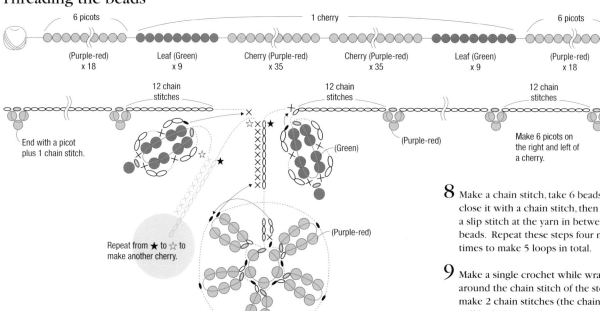

1 Refer to page 84 to measure the size of the section to be edged and calculate the number of motifs and beads required. The final size of the edging can be adjusted with the number of picots or chain stitches.

2 Thread the beads onto the yarn as shown above and make a chain stitch.

3 Make a picot. Take 3 beads and close it with a chain stitch to make a picot, and make 12 chain stitches. Repeat these steps until the required number of picots are made.

4 Make a leaf. Make a chain stitch, take 8 beads and close it with a chain stitch.

5 Make 2 chain stitches, and make a single crochet at the yarn in between the beads. Repeat these steps (these chain stitches will be hidden behind the beads).

6 Take 1 bead and make a chain stitch to fix it, then make a single crochet. Repeat step 5 (make a slip stitch last) and make a single crochet while wrapping around the chain stitch in step 4.

7 Make a cherry. Make 12 chain stitches for a stem (3 stitches will be hidden in the next cherry), take 5 beads and close it with a chain stitch.

8 Make a chain stitch, take 6 beads and close it with a chain stitch, then make a slip stitch at the yarn in between the beads. Repeat these steps four more times to make 5 loops in total.

9 Make a single crochet while wrapping around the chain stitch of the stem, and make 2 chain stitches (the chain stitches will be hidden in the cherry).

10 Collect the center of the loops of 6 beads in step 8 with a slip stitch to make it three-dimensional. After drawing the yarn through the 5th loop, insert the chain stitches as a stem in the cherry, and draw it through the center of the 1st loop to close it.

11 Make 9 single crochets using the chain stitches as a stem.

12 Repeat steps 7 to 11 to make another cherry. Then make a leaf, and make a single crochet while wrapping around the yarn in between the stems (see ☆ and ★).

13 Make 12 chain stitches and make required number of picots. End with a picot.

66

design-3

Fresh German Chamomile Flowers

Beaded edging for a camisole

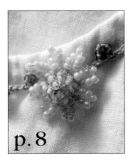

p. 8

- 1 motif: Approx. 6cm (2 3/8") in length, 1.8cm (3/4") in width
- Edging: Approx. 90cm (35 3/8") (15 motifs)

Material	Type/Product No. (color)	Amount used	
		1 motif	Total
Yarn	Olympus #40 No.228 (lime green)	Approx. 100cm (39 3/8")	Approx. 15m (49' 2 1/2")
Beads	Round, No.246 (moss green)	25	375
	Round, No.974 (yellow)	28	420
	Round, No.121 (white)	64	960
Needle	Crochet hook, No. 10 (0.75mm)	–	–

* The length of yarn and the size of motif in the table are for reference only. Allow 20 to 30cm (7 to 12") of yarn for finishing.

* Refer to page 84 to calculate the number of motifs required and thread the beads.

Threading the beads

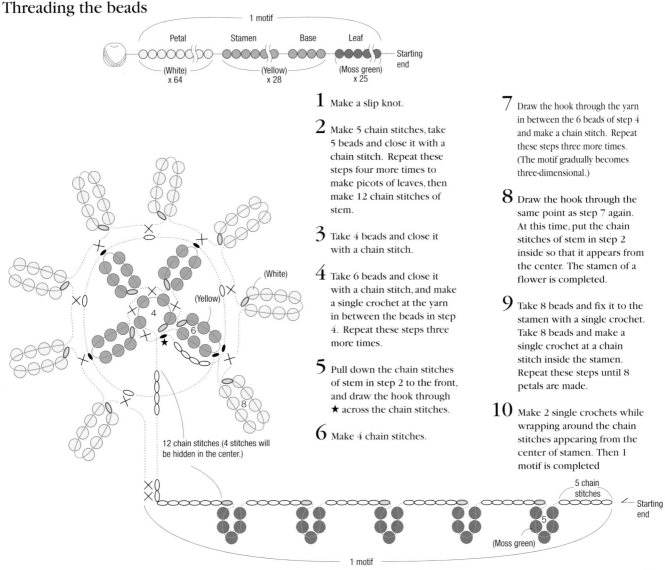

1 motif

Petal — Stamen — Base — Leaf

(White) x 64   (Yellow) x 28   (Moss green) x 25

Starting end

1 Make a slip knot.

2 Make 5 chain stitches, take 5 beads and close it with a chain stitch. Repeat these steps four more times to make picots of leaves, then make 12 chain stitches of stem.

3 Take 4 beads and close it with a chain stitch.

4 Take 6 beads and close it with a chain stitch, and make a single crochet at the yarn in between the beads in step 4. Repeat these steps three more times.

5 Pull down the chain stitches of stem in step 2 to the front, and draw the hook through ★ across the chain stitches.

6 Make 4 chain stitches.

7 Draw the hook through the yarn in between the 6 beads of step 4 and make a chain stitch. Repeat these steps three more times. (The motif gradually becomes three-dimensional.)

8 Draw the hook through the same point as step 7 again. At this time, put the chain stitches of stem in step 2 inside so that it appears from the center. The stamen of a flower is completed.

9 Take 8 beads and fix it to the stamen with a single crochet. Take 8 beads and make a single crochet at a chain stitch inside the stamen. Repeat these steps until 8 petals are made.

10 Make 2 single crochets while wrapping around the chain stitches appearing from the center of stamen. Then 1 motif is completed

(White)

(Yellow)

4

6

8

12 chain stitches (4 stitches will be hidden in the center.)

5 chain stitches

Starting end

5

(Moss green)

1 motif

Honeybees

Beaded edging for a necklace

• 1 motif: Approx. 1.5cm (5/8") in length and width

Material	Type/Product No. (color)	Amount used
		Total
Yarn	Kanagawa Oya Thread (for crochet hook) No.8 (brown)	Approx. 50m (164' 1/2")
Beads	Round, No.221 (dark gold)	32
	Round, matte No.22 (gold)	24
	Round, No.22 (gold)	22
Needle	Crochet hook, No.12 (0.6mm)	–

* The length of yarn and the size of motif in the table are for reference only. Allow 20 to 30cm (7 to 12") of yarn for finishing.

* Refer to page 84 to calculate the number of motifs required and thread the beads.

Threading the beads

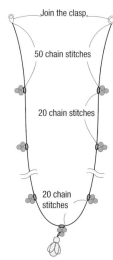

[Necklace] Approx. 1m (39 3/8") in length
Yarn: Olympus #40/No.813 (Beige)
Beads: Round, No.246 (Moss green) x 63
❶ Thread the 63 beads.
❷ Make a slip knot and 50 chain stitches.
❸ Close 3 beads with a chain stitch, and make 20 chain stitches. Repeat these steps until 21 picots are made.
❹ Make 50 chain stitches.
❺ Join the honeybee motif to the picot in the middle, and take care of the yarn end by hiding it inside the motif.

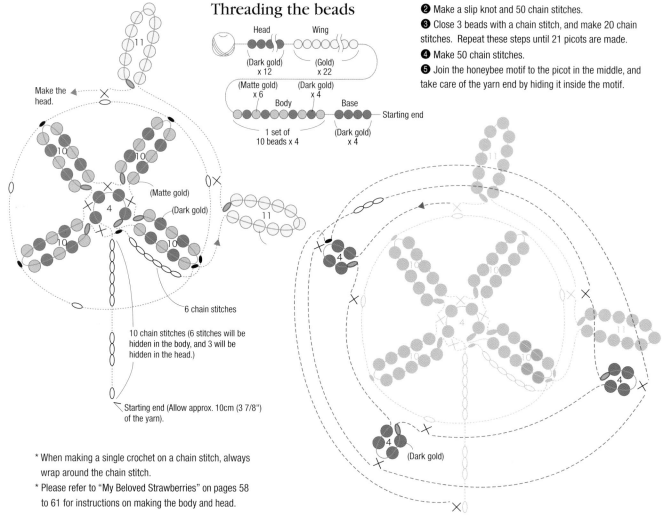

* When making a single crochet on a chain stitch, always wrap around the chain stitch.

* Please refer to "My Beloved Strawberries" on pages 58 to 61 for instructions on making the body and head.

design-5
Bashful Little Roses

Beaded edging for a blouse

p. 10

- 1 motif: Approx. 11.5cm (4 1/2") in length, 1.5cm (5/8") in width
- Size of edging (8 motifs): Approx. 92cm (36 1/4")

Material	Type/Product No. (color)	Amount used		
		1 motif	10 motifs	Total
Yarn	DMC Cebelia #30 No.816 (burgundy)	Approx. 1.98m (6' 6")	Approx. 19.8m (64' 11 1/2")	Approx. 15.9m (52' 2")
Beads	Round, No.959 (pink)	42	420	336
	Round, No.22 (gold)	18	180	144
	Round, No.947 (green)	20	200	160
	Round, No.939 (dark green)	9	90	72
Needle	Crochet hook, No. 10 (0.75mm)	–	–	–

* The length of yarn and the size of motif in the table are for reference only. Allow 20 to 30cm (7 to 12") of yarn for finishing.

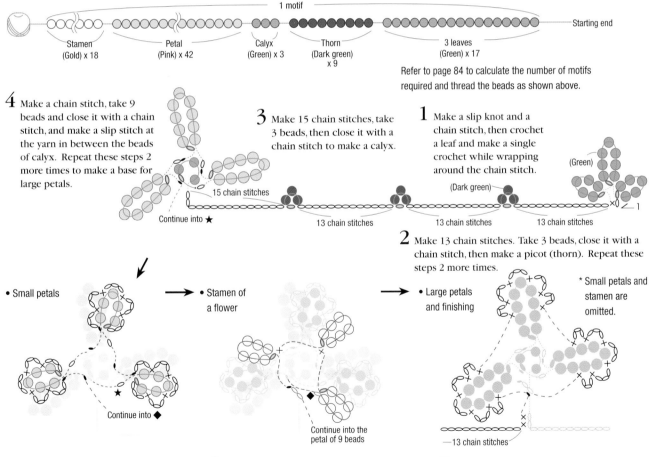

1 motif

Stamen (Gold) x 18 Petal (Pink) x 42 Calyx (Green) x 3 Thorn (Dark green) x 9 3 leaves (Green) x 17 Starting end

Refer to page 84 to calculate the number of motifs required and thread the beads as shown above.

4 Make a chain stitch, take 9 beads and close it with a chain stitch, and make a slip stitch at the yarn in between the beads of calyx. Repeat these steps 2 more times to make a base for large petals.

15 chain stitches

Continue into ★

3 Make 15 chain stitches, take 3 beads, then close it with a chain stitch to make a calyx.

1 Make a slip knot and a chain stitch, then crochet a leaf and make a single crochet while wrapping around the chain stitch.

(Green)

(Dark green)

13 chain stitches   13 chain stitches   13 chain stitches

×0 ⌐1

2 Make 13 chain stitches. Take 3 beads, close it with a chain stitch, then make a picot (thorn). Repeat these steps 2 more times.

- Small petals

Continue into ◆

- Stamen of a flower

Continue into the petal of 9 beads

- Large petals and finishing

* Small petals and stamen are omitted.

—13 chain stitches

5 Make a chain stitch, take 5 beads and close it with a chain stitch, make a loop of 3 chain stitches, then make a slip stitch at the yarn in between the beads of calyx. Repeat these steps 2 more times.

6 Make a chain stitch, take 6 beads and close it with a chain stitch, then make a single crochet at the yarn in between the petals. Repeat these steps 2 more times. (Finish with a slip stitch instead of a single crochet when you make the 3rd one.) Make 2 chain stitches as a bridge to the reverse side .

7 Make a single crochet at the yarn in between the beads of the large petal, and make a loop of 3 chain stitches on 5 beads, respectively. Make a slip stitch at the 2 chain stitches in step 6 and make 2 single crochets while wrapping around the chain stitches of the stem. Then make 13 chain stitches and 1 motif is completed.

Sweet-Colored Sugar Candies

Camisole

p. 14

• 1 motif: Approx. 9mm (3/8") • Size of edging (33 motifs): Approx. 30.5cm (12")

Material	Type/Product No. (color)	Amount used		
		1 motif	1 repeat	Total (33 motifs)
Yarn	DMC Cebelia #40 No.5200 (white)	Approx. 40.5cm (16")	Approx. 2.5m (98 3/8")	Approx. 13.4m (43' 11 1/2")
Beads	Round, No.170 (clear-blue)	6	36	198+4
	Round, No.121 (white)	18	54	306
	Round, No.143 (blue)	18	18	85
	Round, No.905 (pink)	18	18	85
	Round, No.148 (yellow)	18	18	102
Needle	Crochet hook, No. 10 (0.75mm)	–	–	–

* The length of yarn and the size of motif in the table are for reference only. Allow 20 to 30cm (7 to 12") of yarn for finishing.

Threading the beads

Refer to page 84 to calculate the number of motifs required and thread the beads considering the number and the order.

Since 4 colors are used for the 2nd row, use a beading needle. (Please refer to page 45 for instructions.)

• Order of threading the beads for 1 repeat
1st row: Clear-blue x 36 plus 4 for ending
2nd row: White x 18 → Yellow x 18 → White x 18 → Pink x 18 → White x 18 → Blue x 18

1st row

Clear-blue beads for ending x 4

Clear-blue beads x 36

Starting end

1 repeat

2nd row

1 repeat

White x 18 — Yellow x 18 — White x 18 — Pink x 18 — White x 18 — Blue x 18 — Starting end

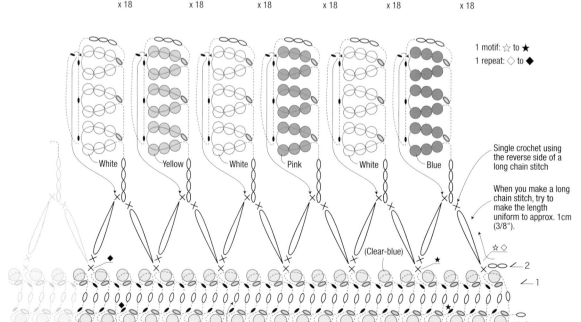

1 motif: ☆ to ★
1 repeat: ◇ to ◆

White · Yellow · White · Pink · White · Blue

Single crochet using the reverse side of a long chain stitch

When you make a long chain stitch, try to make the length uniform to approx. 1cm (3/8").

(Clear-blue)

Crochet 4 extra beads at the end.

* When you crochet the 1st row, turn the crocheted fabric around.
(Turn the fabric around to the same direction every time.)

◆ Make the border of the 1st row.

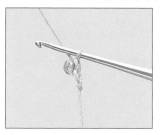
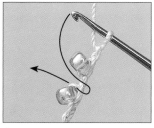

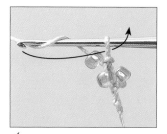

1 Make a starting stitch and a chain stitch, then take 1 bead and close it with a chain stitch.

2 Make a chain stitch, and take 1 bead and close it with a chain stitch, then make 1 more chain stitch. Insert the hook into the stitch closing the first bead as shown above.

3 Wrap the yarn over the hook and make a slip stitch.

4 Take 1 bead and close it with a chain stitch, then make 1 more chain stitch.

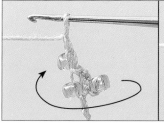

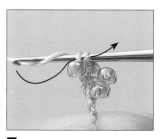
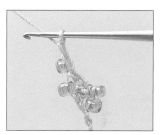

5 Turn the crocheted fabric around. (Turn the fabric around to the same direction every time.)

6 The fabric is turned around.

7 Make a slip stitch using the stitch that closed the previous bead.

8 Take 1 bead and close it with a chain stitch, then make 1 more chain stitch.

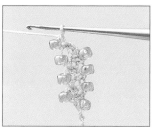
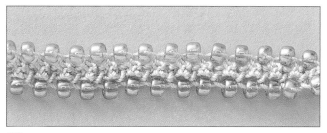

9 Repeat steps 5 to 8 to the required length.

10 Crochet 4 extra beads at the end and cut the yarn.

A border of the 1st row is completed!

◆ Join the yarn for the 2nd row.

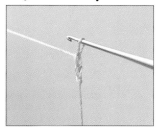

11 Thread the beads for the 2nd row (see page 70). Make a slip knot and 2 chain stitches.

12 Make a single crochet using the stitch closing the 1st bead of the 1st row. Then the yarn for the 2nd row is joined to the 1st row.

Knot stitch

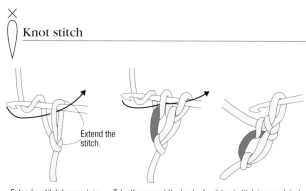

Extend the stitch.

Extend a stitch to a certain length and make a chain stitch.

Take the yarn at the back of the chain stitch, wrap it over the hook and draw the hook through the hook. Wrap the yarn over the hook again and draw the hook through 2 loops.

1 knot stitch is completed.

◆ Knot stitch (See page 71)

13 Draw the loop up over the hook to extend the loop to 1cm (3/8") and make a chain stitch (left). Take the yarn at the back of the chain stitch, wrap it over the hook and draw the hook (center). Wrap the yarn over the hook and draw the hook through all loops (right).

14 One knot stitch is completed.

15 Make 4 chain stitches. Three of them will be hidden in the drop motif to be made next.

◆ Make a drop.

16 Take 6 beads and close it with a chain stitch.

17 A loop of 6 beads is made. Repeat the steps to make 3 loops in total.

18 3 loops are made.

19 Make 3 chain stitches.

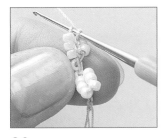

20 Make a slip stitch at the center of the 3rd loop (in between the 3rd and 4th beads).

21 Make a slip stitch at the center of the 2nd loop.

22 In the same way, make a slip stitch at the center of the 1st loop.

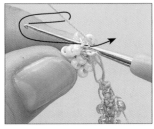

23 Insert the chain stitches in step 15 in the drop motif, then make a slip stitch at the same point as step 20 to close the motif.

◆ Make knot stitches.

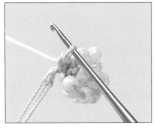

24 Make a single crochet using the chain stitch getting out of the drop motif.

25 Extend the stitch in step 24 and make a knot stitch, then join it to the 1st row with a single crochet. Repeat steps 13 to 25 to the end.

Completed!

Summer-Colored Scabiosa

Beaded edging for a blouse

p. 16

- 1 motif: Approx. 8.7cm (3 3/8") in length / Approx. 2.4cm (1") in width
- Length of edging (16 motifs): Approx. 133cm (4' 4 3/8")

Material	Type/Product No. (color)	Amount used		
		1 motif	1 repeat	Total
Yarn	DMC Cebelia #30 No. 799 (aqua)	Approx. 183cm (6')	Approx. 7.32m (24' 1/4")	Approx. 29.2m (95' 9 5/8")
Beads	Flower A: – Inner petal: Round, No. 954 (green) / Outer petal: Round, No.264 (turquoise blue)	Outer: 55 Inner: 99	Outer: 55 Inner: 99	Outer: 220 Inner: 396
	Flower B: – Inner petal: Round, No. 264 (turquoise blue) / Outer petal: Round, No. 168 (pale blue)		Outer: 55 Inner: 99	Outer: 220 Inner: 396
	Flower C: – Inner petal: Round, No. 172 (light green) / Outer petal: Round, No. 264 (turquoise blue)		Outer: 55 Inner: 99	Outer: 220 Inner: 396
	Flower D: – Inner petal: Round, No. 168 (pale blue) / Outer petal: Round, No. 934 (violet-blue)		Outer: 55 Inner: 99	Outer: 220 Inner: 396
	Leaves: Round, No.558 (platinum)		84	315
Others	Plastic rings for crochet (Outside diameter: 8mm)	9	4	16
Needle	Crochet hook, No. 10 (0.75mm)	–	–	–

Total numbers of beads used:
No.954 (green): 220
No. 264 (turquoise blue): 1,012
No. 172 (light green): 220
No. 934 (violet-blue): 396

* The length of yarn and the size of motif in the table are for reference only. Allow 20 to 30cm (7 to 12") of yarn for finishing.

* Refer to page 84 to calculate the number of motifs required and thread the beads.

Threading the beads

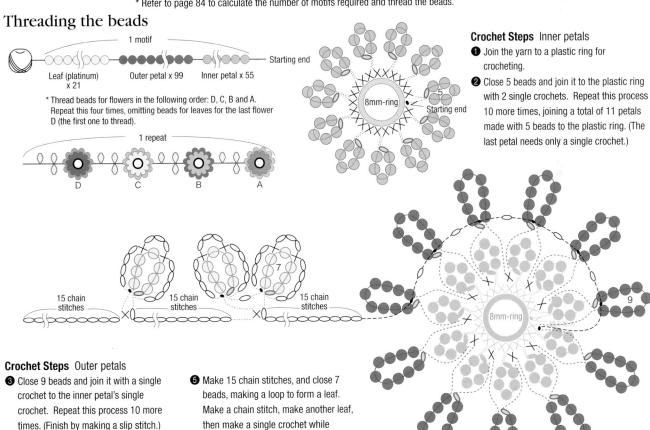

1 motif

Leaf (platinum) x 21 — Outer petal x 99 — Inner petal x 55 — Starting end

* Thread beads for flowers in the following order: D, C, B and A.
Repeat this four times, omitting beads for leaves for the last flower D (the first one to thread).

1 repeat

D   C   B   A

Crochet Steps Inner petals

❶ Join the yarn to a plastic ring for crocheting.

❷ Close 5 beads and join it to the plastic ring with 2 single crochets. Repeat this process 10 more times, joining a total of 11 petals made with 5 beads to the plastic ring. (The last petal needs only a single crochet.)

8mm-ring   5   Starting end

8mm-ring   9

15 chain stitches   15 chain stitches   15 chain stitches   7

Crochet Steps Outer petals

❸ Close 9 beads and join it with a single crochet to the inner petal's single crochet. Repeat this process 10 more times. (Finish by making a slip stitch.)

❹ Repeat the following process for all the outer petals: Make a slip stitch to the chain stitch closing the beads for an outer petal and make a chain stitch. Then pass the yarn to the reverse side of the starting end.

❺ Make 15 chain stitches, and close 7 beads, making a loop to form a leaf. Make a chain stitch, make another leaf, then make a single crochet while wrapping around the 15 chain stitches.

❻ Make 15 chain stitches, make a leaf in the same way as step 5, then make another 15 stitches to complete 1 motif.

❼ Repeat steps ❶ to ❻ to the required length and finish by crocheting a flower.

Fanciful Butterflies

p. 18

Necklace

- 1 motif: Approx. 8.7cm (3 3/8") in length / Approx. 2.5cm (1") in width
- Length (3 motifs): Approx. 16cm (6 1/4")

Material	Type/Product No. (color)	Amount used	
		1 motif	Total
Yarn	Olympus #40 No.813 (beige)	Approx. 130cm (4' 3 1/8")	Approx. 4m (13' 1 1/2")
Beads	idola Jujube Bead – A: 6mm (red) / B: 6mm (blue)	4	12
	idola Jujube Bead – A: 6mm (pink) / B: 6mm (mint)	4	12
	idola JFF 108 (white) – Common	44	132
Needle	Crochet hook, No. 10 (0.75mm)	–	–

* The length of yarn and the size of motif in the table are for reference only. Allow 20 to 30cm (7 to 12") of yarn for finishing.
* Refer to page 84 to calculate the number of motifs required and thread the beads.

Threading the beads

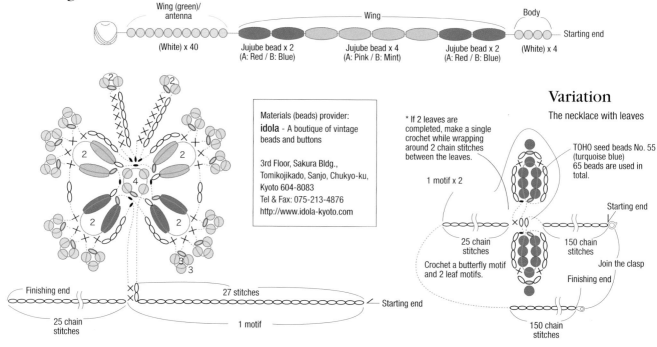

Wing (green)/ antenna

(White) x 40

Jujube bead x 2 (A: Red / B: Blue)

Wing

Jujube bead x 4 (A: Pink / B: Mint)

Jujube bead x 2 (A: Red / B: Blue)

Body

(White) x 4

Starting end

Materials (beads) provider:
idola - A boutique of vintage beads and buttons

3rd Floor, Sakura Bldg.,
Tomikojikado, Sanjo, Chukyo-ku,
Kyoto 604-8083
Tel & Fax: 075-213-4876
http://www.idola-kyoto.com

Variation

The necklace with leaves

* If 2 leaves are completed, make a single crochet while wrapping around 2 chain stitches between the leaves.

1 motif x 2

25 chain stitches

Crochet a butterfly motif and 2 leaf motifs.

TOHO seed beads No. 55 (turquoise blue) 65 beads are used in total.

Starting end

150 chain stitches

Join the clasp

Finishing end

150 chain stitches

Finishing end

25 chain stitches

27 stitches

1 motif

Starting end

1. Make a slip knot.

2. Body: Make 27 chain stitches. Take 4 beads and close them with a chain stitch.

3. Wing: Make a chain stitch, take 2 jujube beads, close them with a chain stitch, then join it with a slip stitch to the yarn between 2 beads of the body in step 2. Repeat this process 3 more times.

4. The edging of the wing: Make 4 chain stitches, then make a single crochet, using the yarn between the jujube beads in step 2.

5. Close 3 beads with a chain stitch, then make a single crochet, using the same yarn as in step 4. Repeat this process 2 more times.

6. Make 2 chain stitches and then a single crochet, using the yarn between the next jujube beads. Repeat step 5 once, make 4 chain stitches and join them with a slip stitch to the yarn between 2 beads of the body in step 2.

7. Antenna: Make 6 chain stitches and close 2 beads with a chain stitch. Make 6 single crochets in the direction of the body while wrapping around the 6 chain stitches, then join them with a slip stitch to the same point as step 6.

8. Repeat step 7 once.

9. Repeat steps 4 to 6 once.

10. Make 2 single crochets while wrapping around the chain stitches in step 2. 1 motif is then completed.

11. Repeat steps 2 to 9 to the required length, then finish with 25 chain stitches.

design-10

Popping Soap Bubbles

Beaded edging for a tunic

p.19

- 1 motif: Approx. 5cm (2") in length / Approx. 3.2cm (1 1/4") in width
- Length of edging (10 motifs): Approx. 50cm (19 5/8")

Material	Type/Product No. (color)	Amount used	
		1 motif	Total
Yarn	DMC Cebelia #40, No.712 (cream)	Approx. 3.1m (10' 2")	Approx. 31m (101' 8 1/2")
Beads	Round, No.45 (red)	63	630
Needle	Crochet hook, No. 10 (0.75mm)	-	-

* The length of yarn and the size of motif in the table are for reference only. Allow 20 to 30cm (7 to 12") of yarn for finishing.
* Refer to page 84 to calculate the number of motifs required and thread the beads.

Threading the beads

1 motif

(Red) x 63 → Starting end

* When making a single crochet on chain stitches, always wrap around the chains.

[Fly]
- 1 motif: Approx. 1.3cm (1/2") in length
- The length of edging (22 motifs): Approx. 27.5cm (10 7/8")
- Amount used: 1 motif:
  Yarn: Approx. 44cm (17 3/8")
  Beads: 7
  Yarn: Approx. 9.7m (31' 9 7/8")
  Beads: 154
Crochet ❶ and ❷ first, then repeat ❷ to the required length. Finish with 8 chain stitches.

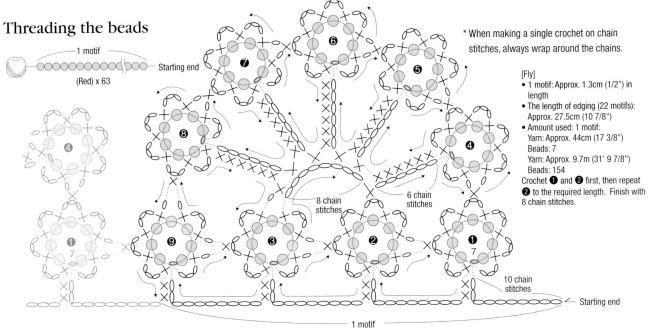

8 chain stitches
6 chain stitches
10 chain stitches
Starting end
1 motif

Steps
Step: When joining the adjacent loop, pay close attention to the direction of turning the crochet work around.

1 After making the first loop, make a chain stitch, turn only the previous motif around, then insert the hook into the center of the 6th loop.

2 Make a single crochet while wrapping around the loop of chain stitches to joining the loops.

3 Turn the crochet work around and make a chain stitch.

4 Pull up the bead loop and make a single crochet at the yarn between beads.

5 The 1st and 2nd loops are joined. Also join the other loops.

Arabesque

Beaded edging for a dress

p. 22

- 1 motif: Approx. 3cm (1 1/8") in length / Approx. 2.5cm (1") in width
- Length of edging for neckline (22 motifs and ends): Approx. 68cm (26 3/4")

Material	Type/Product No. (color)	Amount used		
		1 motif	End	Total
Yarn	Olympus #40 No.731 (natural white)	Approx. 1.6m (5' 3")	Approx. 1.6m (5' 3")	Approx. 36.8m (120' 8 7/8")
Beads	Round, No.552 (pink)	24	18	546
	Round, No.558 (silver)	9	7	205
	Round, No.557 (gold)	3	-	66
Needle	Crochet hook, No. 10 (0.75mm)	–	–	–

* The length of yarn and the size of motif in the table are for reference only. Allow 20 to 30cm (7 to 12") of yarn for finishing.

* Refer to page 84 to calculate the number of motifs required and thread the beads.

Threading the beads

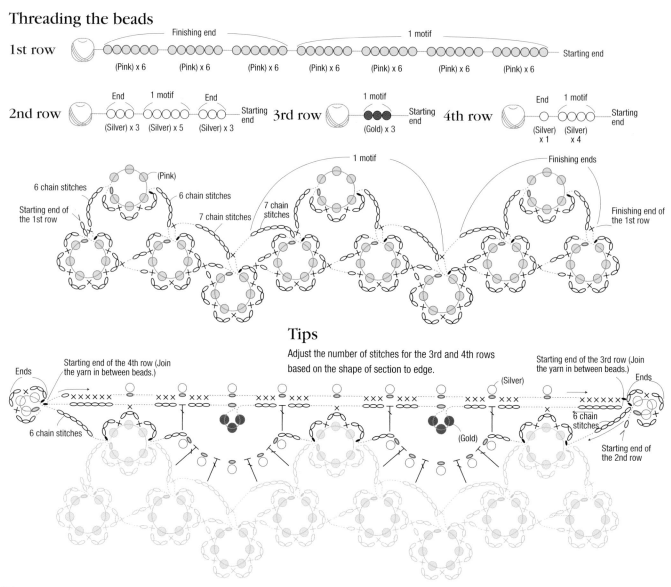

1st row

Finishing end — 1 motif

(Pink) x 6 (Pink) x 6 (Pink) x 6 (Pink) x 6 (Pink) x 6 (Pink) x 6 (Pink) x 6

Starting end

2nd row

End / 1 motif / End / Starting end

(Silver) x 3 (Silver) x 5 (Silver) x 3

3rd row

1 motif / Starting end

(Gold) x 3

4th row

End / 1 motif / Starting end

(Silver) x 1 (Silver) x 4

6 chain stitches (Pink) 6 chain stitches

Starting end of the 1st row

7 chain stitches

7 chain stitches

1 motif

7 chain stitches

Finishing ends

Finishing end of the 1st row

Tips

Adjust the number of stitches for the 3rd and 4th rows based on the shape of section to edge.

Ends

Starting end of the 4th row (Join the yarn in between beads.)

(Silver)

Starting end of the 3rd row (Join the yarn in between beads.)

Ends

6 chain stitches

(Gold)

6 chain stitches

Starting end of the 2nd row

Mandarin Oranges and Blossoms

Beaded edging for a crocheted vest

p. 24

- 1 motif: Approx. 3cm (1 1/8") in length / Approx. 2.5cm (1") in width
- Length of edging (12 motifs and 2 leaves): Approx. 136cm (53 1/2")

Material	Type/Product No. (color)	Amount used		
		1 motif	10 motifs	Total
Yarn	Kanagawa Leather Sewing Hemp Thread, Fine (beige)	Approx. 2.3m (90 1/2")	Approx. 23m (75' 5 1/2")	Approx. 28.5m (93' 6")
Beads	Round, No.175 (yellow) ⎤ Use one of these colors for a motif.	68	680	408
	Round, No.174 (orange) ⎦	68	680	408
	Round, No.167 (green)	24	240	304
	Round, No.401 (white)	30	300	360
	Round, No.974 (matt yellow)	20	200	240
Needle	Crochet hook, No. 10 (0.75mm) (No.8 is also usable.)	–	–	–

* The length of yarn and the size of motif in the table are for reference only. Allow 20 to 30cm (7 to 12") of yarn for finishing.

* Refer to page 84 to calculate the number of motifs required and thread the beads.

Threading the beads

1 motif

2 leaves

(Green) x 8   (Green) x 8   Stamen (Matt yellow) x 15   Petal (White) x 30   Calyx (Matt yellow) x 5

1 leaf (Green) x 8   Fruit (Yellow) x 68 / (Orange) x 68
* Thread yellow and orange beads alternately by motif.   2 leaves (Green) x 8   (Green) x 8   Starting end

1 motif   The first motif

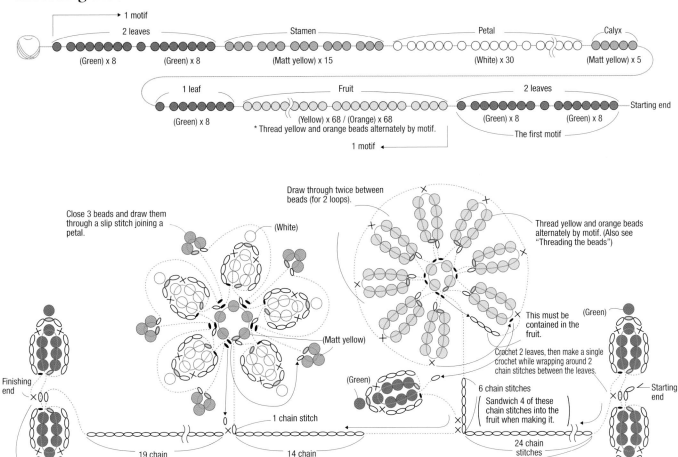

Draw through twice between beads (for 2 loops).

Close 3 beads and draw them through a slip stitch joining a petal.

(White)

Thread yellow and orange beads alternately by motif. (Also see "Threading the beads")

(Matt yellow)

(Green)

This must be contained in the fruit.

Crochet 2 leaves, then make a single crochet while wrapping around 2 chain stitches between the leaves.

(Green)

Finishing end

6 chain stitches
Sandwich 4 of these chain stitches into the fruit when making it.

Starting end

1 chain stitch

19 chain stitches   14 chain stitches   24 chain stitches

1 motif

Grapes

p. 26

Beaded edging for a blanket

- Size of the blanket: Approx. 120 x 90cm (47 1/4" x 35 3/8")
- 1 motif: Approx. 7cm (2 3/4") in length / Approx. 5.5cm (2 1/8") in width   • Length of edging (60 motifs): Approx. 4.2m (13' 9 3/8")

Material	Type/Product No. (color)	Amount used		
		1 motif	10 motifs	Total
Yarn	Olympus Emmy Grande Colors No.675 (purple)	Approx. 2.3m (90 1/2")	Approx. 23m (75' 5 1/2")	Approx. 28.5m (93' 6")
	DMC Cotton Pearl #8 No.3346 (green)	Approx. 4.6m (181 1/8")	Approx. 46m (150' 11")	Approx. 277m (908' 9 1/2")
Beads	Round, No.166 (light purple)	27	270	1620
	Round, No.559 (platinum)	14	140	840
Needle	Crochet hook, No. 4 (for Emmy Grande) / No.6 (for DMC Cotton Pearl #8)	–	–	–

* The length of yarn and the size of motif in the table are for reference only. Allow 20 to 30cm (7 to 12") of yarn for finishing.

Threading the beads

- Grape (Purple)

Starting end

(Light purple) x 27

1 Refer to page 84 to calculate the number of motifs required and crochet the grape motifs. Thread beads onto a purple yarn, make a loop of 6 chain stitches, then complete a motif according to the crochet chart of a grape at the lower right.

- Leaf (Green)

1st row

Leaf   Leaf

Starting end

(Platinum)   (Platinum)
x 3   x 3

2 Thread beads onto a green yarn, crochet leaves on the 1st row, then connect grape motifs. On the 2nd row, make the platform of pergola with 8 chain stitches and a single crochet.

- Pergola (Green)

3rd row

Pergola

(Platinum)
x 8

3 On the 3rd row, crochet the pergola, including 2 beads, and on the 4th row, make picots with 3 chain stitches.

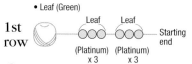

1 motif

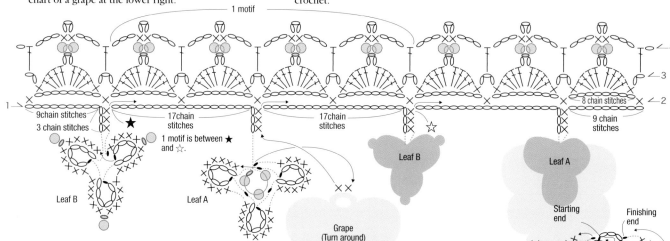

4

3

8 chain stitches

2

9chain stitches

3 chain stitches

17chain stitches

17chain stitches

9 chain stitches

1 motif is between ★ and ☆.

1

Leaf B

Leaf B

Leaf A

Leaf B

Leaf A

Grape (Turn around)

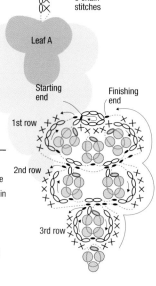

Starting end

Finishing end

1st row

2nd row

3rd row

Steps to crochet a bunch of grapes (Turn the crochet work around to join it with a leaf.)

❶ Start: Make 6 chain stitches, and draw it through the first stitch to make a loop.

❷ The 1st row

Make a chain stitch, close 4 beads with a chain stitch, and make a single crochet, using the loop in Step ❶. Then repeat the following process twice: Make a single crochet, using the loop in Step 1, close 4 beads with a chain stitch, and make a single crochet again, using the loop in Step ❶.

Note: When making a single crochet, wrap around the loop.

❸ Surround the 3 grapes with chain and slip stitches, then make 5 single crochets while wrapping around the 5 chain stitches on the left.

❹ The 2nd row

Close 4 beads with a chain stitch to make a grape and join it to a chain stitch in between the beads in Step ❷. Repeat this process to make one more grape, then surround the 2 grapes in the same manner as Step ❸, then make 5 single crochets while wrapping around the 5 chain stitches on the left.

❺ The 3rd row

Close 4 beads with a chain stitch to make a grape and join it to a chain stitch in between the beads in Step ❹, then make 5 single crochets while wrapping around the 5 chain stitches on the left. Close 3 beads with a chain stitch.

❻ For the grapes in the 3rd row and on the right side in the 2nd and 1st rows, make 5 single crochets while wrapping around the 5 chain stitches on the right, making slip stitches in between the rows. Lastly draw the end through the loop in Step 1 to take care of the yarn end.

Clover

p. 28

Beaded edging for a skirt

- 1 motif: Approx. 2.3cm (7/8") in length / Upper edging (4 rows): Approx. 6cm (2 3/8") in width / Lower edging (6 rows): Approx. 9cm (3 1/2") in width
- Length of edging – Upper (71 motifs): Approx. 163cm (5' 4 1/8") / Lower (78 motifs): Approx. 180cm (5' 10 7/8")

Material	Type/Product No. (color)	Amount used (Upper)		Amount used (Lower)	
		1 motif	Total	1 motif	Total
Yarn	Olympus Emmy Grande Herbs #721 (beige)	Approx. 116.5cm (3' 9 7/8")	Approx. 83m (272' 3 3/4")	Approx. 148.5cm (487' 2 1/2")	Approx. 116m (380' 6 7/8")
Beads	Round, No.108 (green)	18	1278	24	1872
	4-mm round pearl, No.200 (white)	1	71	1	78
Needle	Crochet hook, No. 4	–	–	–	–

*The length of yarn and the size of motif in the table are for reference only. Allow 20 to 30cm (7 to 12") of yarn for finishing.

Threading the beads

- Net pattern

<Upper>
1 motif
Starting end
(Green) x 9

<Lower>
1 motif
Starting end
(Green) x 15

- Clover motif
<Common to Upper and Lower>
1 motif
Starting end
(Green) x 9   (Pearl) x 1

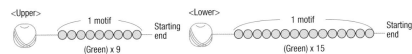

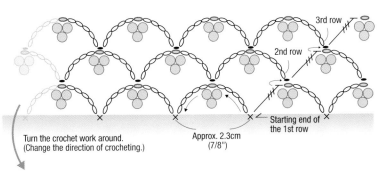

3rd row
2nd row
Starting end of the 1st row
Turn the crochet work around.
(Change the direction of crocheting.)
Approx. 2.3cm (7/8")

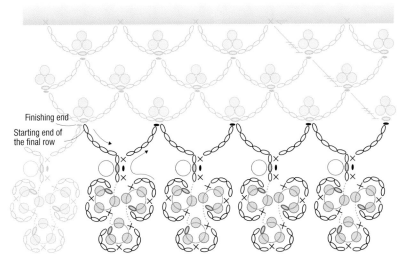

Finishing end
Starting end of the final row

1 Refer to page 84 to calculate the number of motifs required. Prepare extra beads in case the crochet work becomes smaller than the reference size. Please pay attention to the side (front or back) of the crochet work, as you often have to change the direction of crocheting for this piece.

2 The 1st row: Make a slip knot and crochet net patterns, inserting the hook into the fabric at each end of the motif (see page 83). Repeat the following process to the required length: Make 5 chain stitches, close 3 beads with a chain stitch, make 5 more chain stitches, insert the hook into the fabric, then make a single crochet. Finish by making a double treble crochet on the starting end and drawing it through the chain stitch closing the previous group of 3 beads.

3 The 2nd row or upper: Repeat the following process to the required length: Make 5 chain stitches, close 3 beads with a chain stitch, make 5 chain stitches again, then draw it through the chain stitch closing the previous group of 3 beads. Finish by making a double treble crochet on the starting end and drawing it through the chain stitch closing the previous group of 3 beads. Make the required rows, repeating this process.

4 The final row (with clovers): Thread the beads according to the above chart. Turn the crochet work around (to change the direction of crocheting), join the yarn to a chain stitch closing beads on the previous row.

5 Make 6 chain stitches, fix a round pearl with a chain stitch and make a chain stitch to make a petiole. As shown in the left chart, crochet a leaf, closing 3 beads with a chain stitch and making a loop. Then make a single crochet on the petiole, draw it through the chain stitch fixing a round pearl, make a single crochet on the petiole again, make 5 chain stitches, then make a slip stitch to a chain stitch closing beads on the previous row. Repeat this process to the required length and finish by making a slip stitch to the starting end.

Red Hot Peppers

Beaded edging for a tote bag

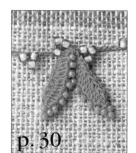

p.30

- 1 motif: Approx. 4cm (1 5/8") in length / Approx. 2.5cm (1") in width
- Length of edging (7 motifs): Approx. 30cm (11 3/4")

Material	Type/Product No. (color)	Amount used	
		1 motif	Total
Yarn	DMC Cebelia #30, No.816 (red)	Approx. 115cm (3' 9 1/4")	Approx. 8.5m (27' 10 5/8")
Beads	Round, No.246 (moss green)	12	84
	Round, No.45 (red)	20	140
Needle	Crochet hook, No. 10 (0.75mm)	–	–

* The length of yarn and the size of motif in the table are for reference only. Allow 20 to 30cm (7 to 12") of yarn for finishing.

* Refer to page 84 to calculate the number of motifs required and thread the beads.

Threading the beads

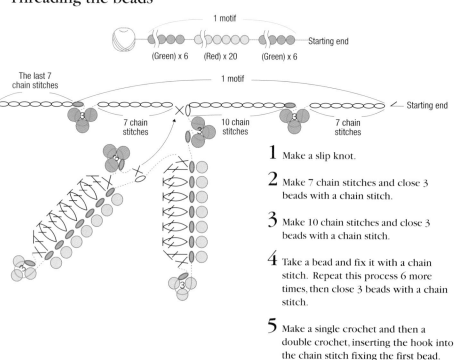

1 motif

(Green) x 6   (Red) x 20   (Green) x 6   Starting end

The last 7 chain stitches

1 motif

7 chain stitches   10 chain stitches   7 chain stitches   Starting end

1 Make a slip knot.

2 Make 7 chain stitches and close 3 beads with a chain stitch.

3 Make 10 chain stitches and close 3 beads with a chain stitch.

4 Take a bead and fix it with a chain stitch. Repeat this process 6 more times, then close 3 beads with a chain stitch.

5 Make a single crochet and then a double crochet, inserting the hook into the chain stitch fixing the first bead.

6 Insert the hook into the chain stitch fixing the next bead and make a cluster with 2 double crochets. Repeat this process 4 more times, then make a double crochet and a single crochet at the chain stitch fixing the last bead.

7 Make a chain stitch, then repeat steps 4 to 6 once.

8 Close 3 beads with a chain stitch, make a single crochet while wrapping around the chain stitch in step 7, then make a single crochet while wrapping around the chain stitch in step 3.

9 Make 7 chain stitches and close 3 beads with a chain stitch.

10 Repeat steps 2 to 9 to the required length and finish by making 7 chain stitches.

p.30: Beaded edging for a girl's dress

Olympus Emmy Grande is used for Flower A; Olympus Emmy Grande or Olympus Crochet Cotton Gold Special #40 for Flower B; DMC Cotton Pearl #8 for Leaves A and B; and TOHO Round Beads No. 559 (gold) for all the beads.

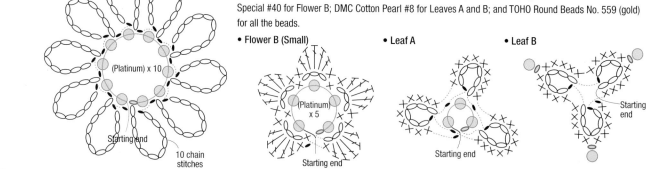

- Flower A (Large)

(Platinum) x 10

Starting end

10 chain stitches

- Flower B (Small)

(Platinum) x 5

Starting end

- Leaf A

Starting end

- Leaf B

Starting end

Turkish Belly Dance

Beaded edging for a scarf

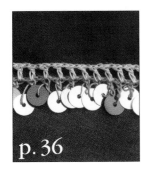

p. 36

- Size of scarf: 90 x 90 cm (2' 11 3/8") • 1 motif: Approx. 2.4cm (1") in length / Approx. 1.2m (3' 11 1/4) in width
- Length of edging (150 motifs): Approx. 360cm (11' 9 3/4)

Material	Type/Product No. (color)	Amount used		
		1 motif	10 motif	Total
Yarn	DMC Special Dantelles #80, No.3778 (dark beige)	Approx. 20cm (7 7/8")	Approx. 2m (6' 6 3/4")	Approx. 30m (98' 5 1/8")
	DMC Special Dantelles #80, No.754 (light beige)	Approx. 22cm (8 5/8")	Approx. 2.2m (7' 2 5/8")	Approx. 33m (108' 3 1/4")
Beads	Spangle, 5mm (Washable) No.2 (gold)	5	50	750
	Spangle, 5mm (Washable) No.7 (purple)	1	10	150
Needle	Crochet hook, No. 10 (0.75mm)	–	–	–

* The length of yarn and the size of motif in the table are for reference only. Allow 20 to 30cm (7 to 12") of yarn for finishing.

* Basting yarn is for securely making double crochet. Prepare thick yarn (around #10) for it. (Length: the length of edging plus approx. 20cm [7 7/8"]).

Threading the spangles

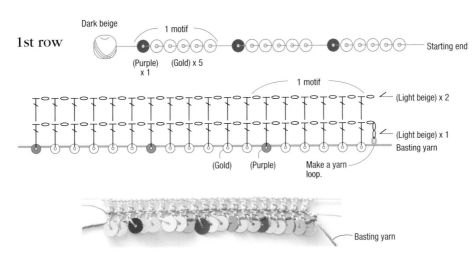

1st row
Dark beige
1 motif
(Purple) x 1
(Gold) x 5
Starting end

1 motif
(Light beige) x 2
(Light beige) x 1
Basting yarn
(Gold) (Purple)
Make a yarn loop.

Basting yarn

Steps
Make double crochets, using basting yarn and including spangles. Sparkling fringes are completed after removing the basting yarn.

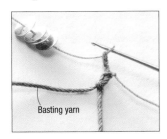

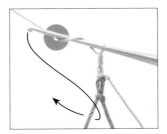

Basting yarn

1 Make a yarn loop that can be undone (see "Make a slip knot." on page 46) and then 3 chain stitches with spangle-threaded yarn.

2 Draw the hook, taking the yarn, then take a spangle and make a double crochet on the basting yarn. Control the length of yarn taken based on the diameter of the spangle to make the size of the stitch uniform.

3 The photo shows a completed double crochet. After this, make a chain stitch, then repeat the following process to the required length: Make a double crochet, including a spangle, then make a chain stitch.

4 Change the yarn for the 2nd row. Repeat the following process to the end: Make a chain stitch, and a double crochet at the double crochet on the 1st row. Finally cut the end of the basting yarn and remove.

Little Bird That Eats Red Fruit

p. 38

Beaded edging for a scarf

- 1 motif: Approx. 5cm (2") in length / Approx. 2m (6' 6 3/4") in width
- Length of edging (72 motifs): Approx. 360cm (11' 9 3/4")

Material	Type/Product No. (color)	Amount used	
		1 motif	Total
Yarn	Olympus #40, No.192 (red)	Approx. 164cm (5' 4 5/8")	Approx. 120m (393' 8 3/8")
Beads	Round, No.401 (white)	17	1224
	Round, No.405 (red)	22	1584
Needle	Crochet hook, No. 10 (0.75mm)	–	–

* The length of yarn and the size of motif in the table are for reference only. Allow 20 to 30cm (7 to 12") of yarn for finishing.

* Refer to page 84 to calculate the number of motifs required and thread the beads.

Threading the beads

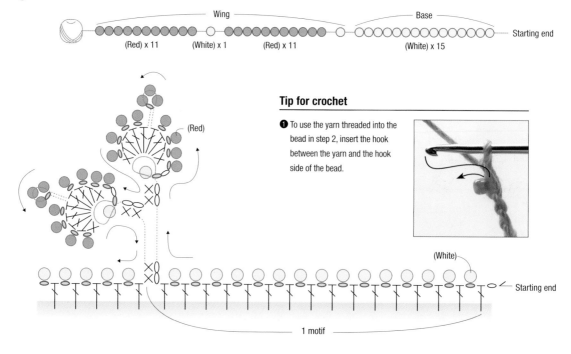

Wing

(Red) x 11   (White) x 1   (Red) x 11

Base

(White) x 15

Starting end

(Red)

Tip for crochet

❶ To use the yarn threaded into the bead in step 2, insert the hook between the yarn and the hook side of the bead.

(White)

Starting end

1 motif

---

1 Make a slip knot and then a chain stitch. Make a double crochet, inserting the hook into the base fabric. Repeat the following process 15 times: Fix a bead with a chain stitch and make a double crochet, inserting the hook into the base fabric. Make 4 chain stitches.

2 Take a bead (white), fix it with a chain stitch, and make a chain stitch.

3 Make a single crochet, a half double crochet and 2 double crochets at the yarn threaded into the bead in step 2 after fixing a bead (red) with a chain stitch each time.

4 Take 3 beads, close them with a chain stitch and make a double crochet at the same section as step 3. Make 2 double crochets, half double crochet, and a single crochet after fixing a bead (red) with a chain stitch each time.

5 Make 2 double crochets while wrapping around 2 of the 4 chain stitches in step 1, then make 2 chain stitches.

6 Repeat steps 2 to 4 once.

7 Make 4 double crochets while wrapping around the 2 chain stitches in step 5 and then the remaining 2 chain stitches in step 1. 1 motif is completed.

8 Repeat steps 1 to 7 to the required length, starting from the process inserting the hook into the base fabric.

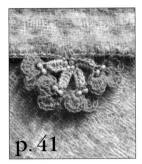

p. 41

design-22
Sun-Soaked Flower Garden

Beaded edging for an autumn-colored stole

- 1 motif: Approx. 12cm (4 3/4") in length / Approx. 2.2cm (7/8") in width
- Length of edging (15 motifs x 2): Approx. 180cm (5' 10 7/8")

Material	Type/Product No. (color)		Amount used		
			1 motif	10 motif	Total
Yarn	DMC Cebelia #30, No.989 (green)		Approx. 1.7m (5' 6 7/8")	Approx. 17m (55' 9 1/4")	Approx. 51m (167' 3 7/8")
	DMC Special Dantelles #80, No.448 (yellow)	Use one of these colors for a motif.	Approx. 2.7m (8' 10 1/4")	Approx. 27m (88' 7")	Approx. 27m (88' 7")
	DMC Special Dantelles #80, No.798 (blue)		Approx. 2.7m (8' 10 1/4")	Approx. 27m (88' 7")	Approx. 27m (88' 7")
	DMC Special Dantelles #80, No.917 (red purple)		Approx. 2.7m (8' 10 1/4")	Approx. 27m (88' 7")	Approx. 27m (88' 7")
Beads	Round, No.559 (Platinum)		18	30	570
Needle	Crochet hook, No. 10 (0.75mm)		–	–	–

* The length of yarn and the size of motif in the table are for reference only. Allow 20 to 30cm (7 to 12") of yarn for finishing.

Threading the beads

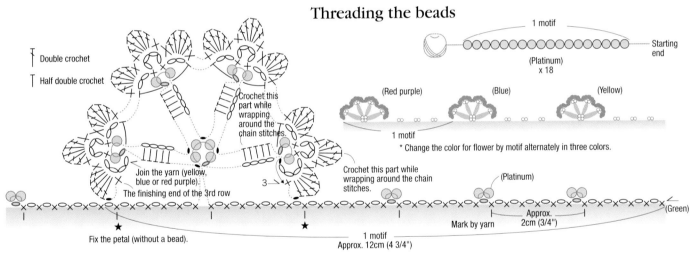

Steps

This is how to crochet, inserting the hook into the fabric directly. On the 1st row, crochet a picot with 2 beads and the stem, then crochet petals using the other yarn, and join them to the stem

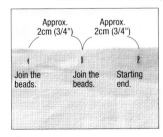

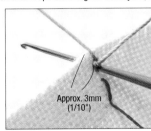

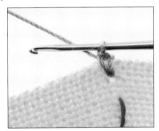

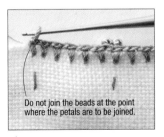

1 Refer to page 84 to calculate the number of motifs required. Iron the fabric and put marks by yarn on points to join beads.

2 Thread beads onto the green yarn and make a slip knot (see page 46). Insert the hook into a point 3mm from the fabric edge.

3 The photo shows the first single crochet made, inserting the hook into the fabric. Then make a chain stitch. Make 6 more single crochets evenly between the marks by yarn.

4 After making the last single crochet at the yarn mark, take 2 beads and close them with a chain stitch. To crochet petals, follow the chart above, starting by closing 4 beads at the base of the stem.

Bright and Lively Scallops

Beaded edging for shoes

- 1 motif: Approx. 0.8cm (1/3") in length / Approx. 1.1cm (2/5") in width
- Length of edging (60 motifs x 2): Approx. 41cm (16 1/8")

p. 34

Material	Type/Product No. (color)	Amount used		
		1 motif	10 motifs	Total
Yarn	Olympus #40, No.192 (dark pink)	Approx. 21cm (8 1/4")	Approx. 63cm (2' 3/4")	Approx. 26m (85' 3 5/8")
Beads	Round, No.954 (aqua)	8	8	176
	Round, No.957 (orange)		8	176
	Round, No.2107 (pink)		8	176
	Round, No.401 (white)	1	3	132
Needle	Crochet hook, No. 10 (0.75mm)	–	–	–

* The length of yarn and the size of motif in the table are for reference only. Allow 20 to 30cm (7 to 12") of yarn for finishing.

* Refer to the following instruction to calculate the number of motifs required and thread the beads.

Threading the beads

1st row

Finish with the half motif

1 repeat

1 motif

(Aqua) x 4   (Pink) x 8   (Orange) x 8   (Aqua) x 8   Starting end

2nd row

a1 repeat

(White) x 1   (White) x 1   (White) x 1   Starting end

Materials for simple decorations on straps are not included in the table above. Prepare 8 beads of Round, No.954 and 32 beads of No.2017.

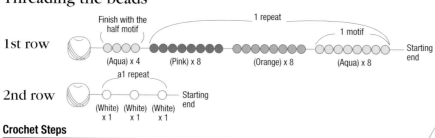

Crochet Steps

❶ The 1st row: Make a slip knot and then a chain stitch.

❷ Take 4 beads and close them with a chain stitch. Repeat this process once more.

❸ Turn the crochet work around, make 2 chain stitches, and make a single crochet at the yarn between beads. Repeat this process 3 more times.

❹ Repeat steps 2 to 3 to the required length.

❺ Finish by taking 4 beads and closing them with a chain stitch.

❺ The 2nd row: Turn the crochet work around, make a chain stitch, then make a single crochet at the yarn between beads in step 2.

❻ Make a chain stitch, fix a bead with a chain stitch and make a chain stitch.

❼ Repeat steps 6 to 7 to the end.

The ABCs of Edging with Beads

Enjoy remaking your T-shirts, bags, and various goods with beaded edging!

1 Measuring the length of the edging.

Beaded edging can be used for almost anything: the front placket or sleeve edge of a cardigan, the neckline of a blouse or T-shirt, the pockets or hems of jeans, stoles, camisoles, and so on. Once you have decided on the item to be used, measure the length of part to be edged, choose the edging design and prepare the materials needed. If 62.5cm (24 5/8") of edging is needed for a cardigan, divide the length by the length of 1 motif of the chosen design. If 1 motif requires 33 beads, 33 x 12 motifs = 396 beads (plus extra beads for adjustment) are needed. Since the length of a crocheted fabric may be different depending on the individual, prepare enough yarn and beads for 3 to 4 cm more than the calculated quantity as a safety margin.

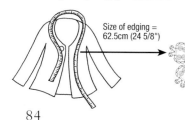

Size of edging = 62.5cm (24 5/8")

design-8
1 motif = 5cm (2")
62.5 ÷ 5cm = 12.5*
* Set the number of motifs as 12 and adjust with picots.

2 Threading beads and crocheting edging.

Thread the required number of beads, along with some extras [for 3 to 4 cm (1-1/8" to 1-3/8")] onto the yarn. When using beads of two or more colors, be careful not to confuse the bead order. After threading the beads, crochet it a bit tightly according to the crochet chart, taking care that the shape and size of each motif is equal.

- When using yarn and beads in different sizes, be sure to crochet as a trial to calculate the required amount and then thread slightly more beads than the required amount.
- When unwanted beads are mixed... Simply break them off with a nipper.
- When running short of yarn... Add new yarn with beads at a less-noticeable point, such as the end of a motif. Do not tie the ends of both pieces of yarn because beads will not pass smoothly over the knot. Insert the end of a piece of yarn into chains or beads to make them less noticeable.
- When running short of beads... Allow 10cm (3-7/8") of yarn and cut it, threading beads on with a clew. Continue crocheting as when running short of yarn and hide the ends. You can also cut the required length of yarn (the last end). In this case, pay attention to the bead order (the reverse order to the first order).

design-23

Dancing Fans

Beaded edging for a change purse

p. 42

- 1 motif: Approx. 1.5cm (3/5") in length / Approx. 1.3cm (1/2") in width

Material	Type/Product No. (color)	Amount used
		1 motif
Yarn	YarnKanagawa Oya Yarn (Tıg)	Approx. 52cm (20 1/2")
Beads	Round	12
Needle	Crochet hook, No. 12	–

* See the list in the lower right for the combination of yarn and beads.
* The length of yarn and the size of motif in the table are for reference only. Allow 20 to 30cm (7 to 12") of yarn for finishing.
* Refer to the following instructions to calculate the number of motifs required and thread the beads.

Crochet Steps

❶ The 1st row: Make 6 chain stitches, close 4 beads with a chain stitch and make 6 chain stitches.

❷ Make 8 double crochets at the yarn between the beads in step 1.

❸ Make a slip stitch at the starting chain stitch (for the second motif or later, the last single crochet of the previous motif).

❹ Repeat the following process to join 8 beads in total: Fix a bead and make a single crochet at the double crochet.

❺ Repeat steps 1 to 4 to the required length, and then the following process for the 2nd row: Make 10 chain stitches and make a single crochet at the chain stitch, closing beads in step 1.

Threading the beads

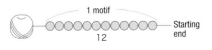

* To sew the edging for a purse:
Be sure to prevent the 2nd row of edging from sagging at the opening of the purse, and sew the edging on the purse body neatly along the seam, preventing the motifs from becoming twisted.

- From the top in page 42:

Yarn: No. 23 (Aqua)   Beads: No. 121 (White)
Yarn: No. 10 (Dark red)   Beads: No. 559 (Gold)
Yarn: No. 14 (Light pink)   Beads: No. 332 (Red purple)
Yarn: No. 31 (Purple)   Beads: No. 552 (Metallic purple)
Yarn: No. 21 (Lemon yellow)   Beads: No. 957 (Orange)
Yarn: No. 8 (Dark brown)   Beads: No. 24 (Lime green)
Yarn: No. 12 (Shocking pink)   Beads: No. 558 (Platinum)

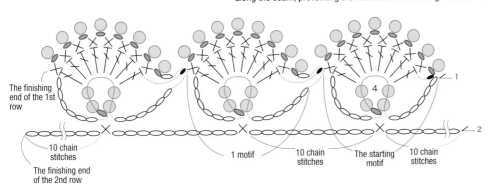

The finishing end of the 1st row

10 chain stitches

The finishing end of the 2nd row

1 motif

10 chain stitches

The starting motif

10 chain stitches

3 Sewing the edging with beads.

Join the finished edging with beads a bit loosely to the edge of the fabric, using dress pins on the fabric as a temporary measure, and finally sew it 3 chains apart. See the instructions at right to sew in a suitable manner for the item.

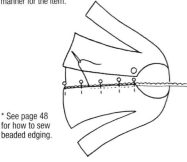

* See page 48 for how to sew beaded edging.

- **Sewing the edging on the front side**
Sew the edging on the front side of the fabric with the same color yarn as that of the chain stitches.

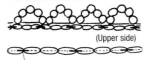

(Upper side)

Running stitch at every 3rd or 4th chain. (Hook the part in between two chains.)

- **Sewing for the appropriate material**
Sew the edging on stretchy material such as knit with a blind stitch, allowing an extra margin of yarn. On the other hand, sew edging onto scarves with a running stitch to avoid sagging.

- **Sewing the edging on the reverse side**
Sew the edging on the reverse side of the fabric with a blind stitch using the same color yarn as the fabric.

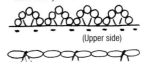

(Upper side)

Blind stitch at every 3rd or 4th chain.

- **Appropriate yarn for sewing**
Special yarn for stretchy materials such as knit is recommended. When using sewing yarn, cut it short, as it becomes twisted easily.

- **Sewing the edging on a border**
Fit the edging on the rim of the fabric and join them with a blind stitch with the same color yarn as that of the chain stitches.

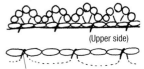

(Upper side)

Blind stitch at every 3rd or 4th chain.

- **Sewing on curved edges**
Sew the edging along the curve with a blind stitch, allowing an extra margin of yarn and preventing the motifs from becoming twisted.

design-11

Spring Mimosa

Beaded edging for a change purse

• 1 motif: Approx. 1.5cm (3/5") in length / Approx. 1.3cm (1/2") in width

Material	Type/Product No. (color)	Amount used		
		First motif	1motif	Total
Yarn	DMC Cebelia #30 No. 989 (green)	Approx. 5cm (2")	Approx. 16.5cm (6 1/2")	Approx. 15.5m (50' 10 1/4")
Beads	Round, No.974 (yellow)	5	5	460
Needle	Crochet hook, No. 10 (0.75mm)	–	–	–

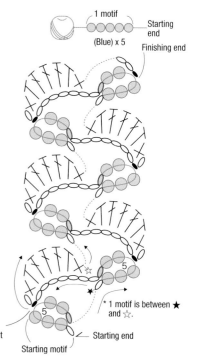

1 motif
Starting motif
Starting end

Threading the beads

Beads for the starting motif

* The length of yarn and the size of motif in the table are for reference only. Allow 20 to 30cm (7 to 12") of yarn for finishing.

1 motif
(Yellow) x 5   (Yellow) x 5   (Yellow) x 5   (Yellow) x 5   Starting end

1 Refer to page 84 to calculate the number of motifs required. Prepare extra beads in case the crochet work ends up smaller than the reference size.

2 Thread beads as shown in the chart above and make a slip knot.

3 Starting motif: Make a chain stitch, close 5 beads with a chain stitch, then make 3 chain stitches.

4 Turn the crochet work around, take 5 beads and close them with a chain stitch.

5 Make 5 double crochets at the yarn between the 2nd and 3rd beads of the 5 beads previously made.

6 Repeat steps 4 to 5 to the required length.

* For all variations on page 20, use DMC Cebelia #30 and round beads.
Edging in Blue – Yarn: No.800 / Beads: No.917 & 920
Edging in Yellow – Yarn: No.745 / Beads: No.164 & 162
Edging in Pink – Yarn: No.842 / Beads: No.332 & 959

---

design-25

Lily of the Valley

Beaded edging for T-shirts

• 1 motif: Approx. 0.6cm (1/5") in length / Approx. 1.5cm (3/5") in width
• Length of edging (56 motifs): Approx. 35cm (13 3/4")

Material	Type/Product No. (color)	Amount used	
		1motif	Total
Yarn	Olympus #40, No.813 (beige)	Approx. 27cm (10 5/8")	Approx. 15.5m (50' 10 1/4")
Beads	Round, No.183 (blue)	5	280
Needle	Crochet hook, No. 10 (0.75mm)	–	–

* The length of yarn and the size of motif in the table are for reference only. Allow 20 to 30cm (7 to 12") of yarn for finishing.
* Refer to page 84 to calculate the number of motifs required and thread the beads.

Threading the beads

1 motif
Starting end
(Blue) x 5   Finishing end

Crochet Steps

❶ Make a slip knot.
❷ Make a chain stitch and close 5 beads with a chain stitch.
❸ Repeat step ❷ once.
❹ Make 7 stitches and then a slip stitch at the yarn between the 3rd and 4th beads of the first motif.

❺ Turn the crochet work around, make a chain stitch, and make a single crochet, half double crochet, 3 single crochets, half double crochet and then a single crochet while wrapping around the chains in step ❹.

❻ Repeat steps ❸ to ❺ to the required length. Finish by making 2 chain stitches, and a slip stitch at the yarn between the beads.

After making a slip stitch between the beads, turn the crochet work around

* 1 motif is between ★ and ☆.

Starting end
Starting motif

86

d e s i g n - 2 1

Yachts on the Waves

Beaded edging for a cloth

A

B

p. 40

- 1 motif: Approx. 4.5cm (1 3/4") in length / Approx. 1.6cm (3/5") in width
- Length of edging (10 motifs): Approx. 47cm (18 1/2")

Material	Type/Product No. (color)	Amount used	
		1 motif	Total
Yarn	DMC Cebelia #30 – A: No.712 (natural white) / B: No.797 (blue)	Approx. 104cm (3' 5")	Approx. 10.5m (34' 5 3/8")
Beads	A: Round, No.712 (blue green) / B: Round, No.122 (white)	6	63
Needle	Crochet hook, No. 10 (0.75mm)	–	–

* The length of yarn and the size of motif in the table are for reference only. Allow 20 to 30cm (7 to 12") of yarn for finishing.

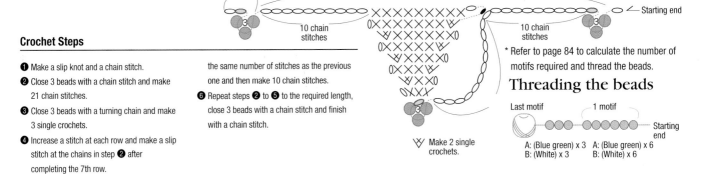

Last motif

1 motif

10 chain stitches

10 chain stitches

Starting end

Make 2 single crochets.

* Refer to page 84 to calculate the number of motifs required and thread the beads.

Threading the beads

Last motif   1 motif

Starting end

A: (Blue green) x 3   A: (Blue green) x 6
B: (White) x 3   B: (White) x 6

Crochet Steps

❶ Make a slip knot and a chain stitch.

❷ Close 3 beads with a chain stitch and make 21 chain stitches.

❸ Close 3 beads with a turning chain and make 3 single crochets.

❹ Increase a stitch at each row and make a slip stitch at the chains in step ❷ after completing the 7th row.

❺ Make a chain stitch, crochet the 8th row with the same number of stitches as the previous one and then make 10 chain stitches.

❻ Repeat steps ❷ to ❺ to the required length, close 3 beads with a chain stitch and finish with a chain stitch.

---

d e s i g n - 2 6

Heart

Beaded edging for T-shirts

p. 49

- 1 motif: Approx. 1.8cm (7/10") in length / Approx. 1.5cm (3/5") in width
- Length of edging (20 motifs): Approx. 35cm (13 3/4")

Material	Type/Product No. (color)	Amount used		
		1 motif	First motif	Total
Yarn	DMC Cebelia #30 No. 746 (cream)	Approx. 80cm (31 1/2")	Approx. 6cm (2 3/8")	Approx. 16m (52' 5 7/8")
Beads	Round, No.125 (red)	22	3	443
Needle	Crochet hook, No. 10 (0.75mm)	–	–	–

* The length of yarn and the size of motif in the table are for reference only. Allow 20 to 30cm (7 to 12") of yarn for finishing.

* Refer to page 84 to calculate the number of motifs required and thread the beads.

Threading the beads

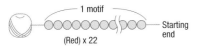

1 motif

(Red) x 22

Starting end

Crochet Steps

❶ Make a loop of 3 beads four times as the base.

❷ Make a loop with chain stitches and double crochets, then repeat the following process to the end: Fix a bead with a chain stitch and make a single crochet.

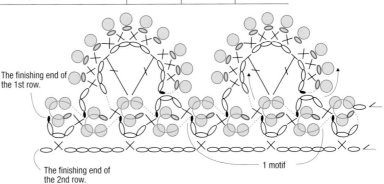

The finishing end of the 1st row.

The finishing end of the 2nd row.

1 motif

Authors

Midori Nishida

Ms. Midori Nishida is a professional craft artist whose work spans a variety of fields. Deeply moved and inspired by the "Turkish Embroideries and Oya Exhibition", she endeavored to create her own line of crafts and introduced Boncuk oya to Japan, adapting it into a more accessible form for Japanese crafters. The cultural exchange tour to Turkey in which she participated in 2006 turned her into a lifelong devotee of oya. She has since continued to study and perfect the art of "beaded edgings" with CRK design, co-author of this book, and has built a massive base of loyal fans both in and outside of Japan. In 2008, she appeared in "Oshare Koubou", an NHK TV craft show, which helped to make "beaded edgings" immensely popular in Japan.

C·R·K design

CRK design is a design firm made up of six graphic designers, Chiaki Kitaya, Kaoru Emoto, Kuma Imamura, Kumiko Yajima, Yasuko Endo, Noriko Yoshiue.
Their first craft magazine design project opened the door to their career in craft making and design. Today, they do everything from designing and production to book designing. In collaboration with Ms. Midori Nishida, co-author of this book, the group has generated an endless stream of creative ideas and designs for decorative edgings.
http://www.crk-design.com/

CRK design has held a number of "beaded edgings" exhibitions mainly in Tokyo and Kyoto, in addition to appearing on TV and sponsoring numerous workshops. They held a workshop at The 10th Nordic Knitting Symposium in July 2009, where the audience, made up of participants from Nordic countries, America and Asia, were swept away by the delicate beauty and charm of beaded edgings.

Profile of CRK design members

Chiaki Kitaya

Graduated from Musashino Art University Junior College of Art and Design. Through her planning and designing role at the Kazuko Endo Design Office, she discovered the joy of coordinating team efforts to create new and innovative products. This inspired her to establish CRK design in 1996.
She is currently in charge of creative and shooting direction, styling, graphic design and production management.

Kaoru Emoto

Graduated from Musashino Art University Junior College of Art and Design, and went on to study professional calligraphy in the U.S. Joined CRK design in 1996 as a founding member. She has designed numerous embroidery charts for craft magazines, and enjoys creating paper crafts applying her lettering & calligraphy skills.

Kuma Imamura

Graduated from Tama Art University. Started her home decor and craft design career at Kazuko Endo Design Office while still a student. Joined CRK design in 2001. She also does editing in addition to her primary role of graphic design. As a skilled knitter and crocheter, she is able to knit and crochet a wide range of items.

Kumiko Yajima

Upon graduating from Tama Art University, she embarked on a career as a mural and background painter, later joining CRK design in 2003. Her exposure to various materials and techniques awakened her interest in craft making. At CRK design, her main responsibilities include production and illustration.

Noriko Yoshiue

Worked for an ad agency as a graphic designer, and later went freelance. While designing craft-related publications, she has been creating patchwork quilts and lace crochet for a membership magazine. Enamored with the beauty of beaded edgings, she pours her heart and soul into her every creation. She is responsible for successfully creating motifs using thick yarn, something which has long been a challenge for crocheters.

Yasuko Endo

Upon graduating from the department of Apparel Design at Joshibi University of Art and Design Junior College, she joined the planning department of an apparel manufacturer, and later turned freelance. She is currently in charge of making craft and home décor products. Awakened to the beauty of Japanese kimono and vintage fabrics, she now takes lessons in Japanese dress-making techniques.

Photographer

Yoshiharu Ohtaki

Graduated from the department of Photography at Kuwasawa Design School. Started freelancing after working as an assistant to a commercial photographer. Held the "Indian Time" exhibition (Nikon Salon) in 1985. Founded studio seek in 1997. He is a member of the Japan Photographers Society, and author of "A Journey into Japanese Textile Dyeing" (Graphic-sha Publishing Co., Ltd.)
http://www.seek-jp.com

Collaborators

Kanji Ishimoto, Chieko Ishimoto

Founded the Japan Turkey Culture Exchange Association in 1993. Is active in promoting person and cultural exchanges between Japan and Turkey to foster friendship between the two nations. Held "Turkish Embroideries and Oya Exhibition" in conjunction with the "2003: Turkey Year in Japan." Mr. and Mrs. Ishimoto are also members of the "Japan Year 2010 in Turkey" executive committee.